The Precarious Center

The PRECARIOUS CENTER

Or

When Will The African Narrative Hold?

MOLEFI KETE ASANTE

Universal Write Publications LLC

No part of this publication may be reproduced in whole or in part, or stored in a retrieval system, or transmitted in any form or by any means, electronic, mechanical, photocopying, recording or otherwise, without written permission from the publisher, except in the case of newspapers, magazines and websites using quotations embodied in critical essays and reviews.

RADICAL INSURGENCIES

Copyright 2020 @ Molefi Kete Asante

All rights reserved.

Molefi Kete Asante
'The right of Molefi Kete Asante to be identified as the author of this Work has been asserted by him/her in accordance with sections 77 and 78 of the Copyright, Designs and Patents Act 1988.'

Book Designer: AuthorSupport.com

For information:
Website at www.UniversalWrite.com and www.UWPBooks.com
Publisher: Universal Write Publications LLC

Mailing/Submissions
Universal Write Publications LLC
421 8th Avenue, Suite 86
New York, NY 10001-9998

ISBN: 978-1-942774-06-8

Selected portions of chapters 1-3 were previously given as speeches. A version of chapter 4 was given as a speech to the Zimbabwe National Museum of Art, Harare, Zimbabwe in September 11-14, 2017. A version of chapter 7 was part of a speech given to the UN General Assembly April 25, 2013.

All ideas are original to the author unless otherwise attributed to others.

Cover art by Nah Dove.

Contents

About the Author ix

Preface xiii

Futures Out of Chaos   1

Eshuean Crossroads   27

Understanding a Federal African State:
An Historical Example   47

African Art and Cognitive Narration   61

Curricula Insurgency   75

In Search of an Afrocentric Historiography   91

Threats to African Peace   11

About the Author

MOLEFI KETE ASANTE

Molefi Kete Asante is an activist intellectual who is President, Molefi Kete Asante Institute for Afrocentric Studies, and Professor and Chair, Department of Africology and African American Studies at Temple University in Philadelphia. He also serves as the International Organizer for Afrocentricity International. Asante is a Guest Professor, Zhejiang University, Hangzhou, China and Professor Extraordinarius at the University of South Africa. Asante, one of the most prolific African American scholars, has published 94 books, among the most recent are *The African American People: A Global History*; *Erasing Racism: The Survival of the American Nation*; *Revolutionary Pedagogy*; *The History of Africa*; *African Pyramids of Knowledge*; *Facing South to Africa*, and, *As I Run Toward Africa*. Asante has published more than 500 articles and is considered one of the most quoted living African authors as well as one of the most distinguished thinkers in the African world. He has been recognized as one of the 10 most widely cited African scholars. *Asante has been* recognized as one of the most influential leaders in education. He completed his BA at Oklahoma Christian, the M.A. at Pepperdine, and received his Ph.D. from the University of California, Los Angeles, at the age of 26, and was appointed a full professor at the age of 30 at the State University of New York at Buffalo. At Temple University he created the first Ph.D. Program in African American Studies in 1988. He has directed more than 135 Ph.D. dissertations making him the top producer of doctorates among African American scholars. He is the founder of the theory of Afrocentricity.

Asante was born in Valdosta, Georgia, of Sudanese (Nubian) and Nigerian (Yoruba) DNA heritage. He is one of sixteen children. He is married to Ana Yenenga, an African Costa Rican, with Akan ancestry via Jamaica. He has three children, Mario, Eka, and MK, Jr., who was born in Zimbabwe. He has six grandchildren, Jamar Ramses, Ayaana, Aion, Nova, Akira, and Akila. He is a poet, novelist, dramatist, and a painter. His works on African language, African history, multiculturalism, and human culture and philosophy have been cited and reviewed by journals such as the *Africalogical Perspectives, Quarterly Journal of Speech, Journal of Black Studies, Journal of Communication, American Scholar, Daedalus, Western Journal of Black Studies*, and *International Journal of Pan African Thought*. The *Utne Reader* called him one of the "100 Leading Thinkers" in America. Asante has appeared on numerous television programs in Africa, Asia, America, and Europe. He is found on all social media. He has received many awards and honors for scholarship and political activism. He regularly consults with heads of state in Africa and has become one of the most popular lecturers on African and African American history and culture. He serves on the Thabo Mbeki African Leadership Council at UNISA and New Haven. Dr.

Asante is the founding editor of the *Journal of Black Studies* (1969) and was the President of the Civil Rights organization, the Student Non-Violent Coordinating Committee's chapter at UCLA in the 1960's. In 1995 he was made a traditional king, Nana Okru Asante Peasah, Kyidomhene (CHEE-DOM-HENI) of Tafo, Akyem, Ghana. He was recently made a Wanadu of the Court of Hassimi Maiga, the Amiru of Gao, Songhay. Asante trained journalists in Zimbabwe immediately after the 2nd Chimurenga and was a mentor to the first group of liberated journalists from Zimbabwe Institute of Mass Communication. He is the International Organizer for Afrocentricity International, a global African organization involved in establishing new pathways to African identity, consciousness, unity, spirituality, and renaissance. Asante has received honorary doctorates and awards from several universities, including Pepperdine, Sojourner Douglass, and New Haven.

Preface

My concern in this book, ***The Precarious Center***, is the degree to which Africans have become enamored through Greek, English, French, German, Spanish, and Portuguese with Westernity to the detriment of African ideas and ideals. Only in the re-centering of the African World in its own narrative subjectivity can true freedom of thought, innovation, and liberation exist as a way to enhance human knowledge. The Pan European Academy with all of its structural capital amassed over the centuries and enshrined in the educational systems of Africans has continued to dominate the theoretical and value base of African inquiries.

The point I make in this preface is that Western notions grounded in the myths and memes of Greek society obliterate all other possibilities and reinforce the idea of European superiority in a multiethnic and multicultural world. In a quest for a broader sense of what the prize-winning africologist Ibram Kendi calls the true intellectual project I want to see a total respect for all cultures. Therefore, in this book I assert the idea that to strengthen global communication equality and free the spirit of humanity we must challenge the assertive memes of the West to allow spaces for a multiplicity of cultural postures.

In a practical sense this means that I want to urge the reader to examine how the memes of Greek and Roman realities are related to those of other classical civilizations in an effort to minimize the aggressive anti-human behavior of those who do not understand the totality of human experience. I am suggesting that it is necessary to be conscious of Zeus while simultaneously discovering in this Greek symbol the psycho-myths that haunt our present time. Of course, I do not project either Ra or Odudua as superior to Zeus, only that they have a seat at the table.

Since linguistic environments are constructed by humans with whatever baggage they bring or whatever they can find in the natural environment, I believe that we can reconstruct or add to environments as needed to expand our understanding. One of the courses I teach at the University is Middle Egyptian and after teaching for so many years I am rarely surprise now to find that many students approach the subject with awe because they have never understood where classical Africa fit in the equation of life. They have some inclinations about Mayans, Chinese, Indians but little knowledge of the African word, either in its ancient of contemporary context.

While it is not precisely the intention of this book to explore all of the ways that the Greek myths have affected us I do think that this is a proper course for those interested in understanding the socially constructed universe. Living in the West or in Africa we often see that city names, street names, the week-days, planets, stars, and even corporations are characteristically Western in orientation and that they are grounded in the names created by Europeans to capture their built environment.

Yet the inquisitive scholar or intellectual wants to expose the way the myths constrain communication across fields such as medicine, sports, and astronomy and to demonstrate how shared myths or a combination of myths and memes can reflect today's multiethnic and different world. As African intellectuals to implement this last objective we need to become aware of how our own myths, social constructions, historical narratives of thinking and acting as homo sapiens in Africa and outside. Some have come to think that the only environment is European. While I think that colonial and imperialism had a lot to do with this I also believe like Cheikh Anta Diop that we can do a lot to change this in our own African minds if we knew our own histories. To correct this situation requires a more robust education, something that emerged with the ethnic studies movement in American universities, but this must become pervasive in Africa.

The common nicknames for schools and hotels in the United States such as Athenas, Athenaeum, Athenians, Argonauts, Centaurs, Golden Griffins, Golden Rams, Griffins, Griffons, Phoenix, Titans, Trojans, Spartans, and so forth are reflective of the built environment. Furthermore, Words and Terms that undergird the ethnocentric environment such as Achilles heel, Trojan horse, Stentorian roar, Myrmidons, Troy, Scylla and Charybdis, and siren voices constitute a veritable canopy of symbols with no space for others. One sees how this is augmented by ideas such as *a Cassandra* or *a Mentor* that are derived from the same rich Greek and Roman classical environment as other memes of culture. How to educate ourselves and our students so that we are comfortable with other memes or myths from other cultures is the challenge of the next generation. What do we make of the space that is covered by names such as Atlas, Clotho,

Cronos. Eros,. Fortuna, Hypno, Chaos, Mars, Mercury, Narcissus, Calypso, Nymphs, Typhon, Vulcan, and Zephyr?

According to Plato this name Atlas was also the name given to the first king of Atlantis although this person is not identified as a son of Zeus, but rather the son of Poseidon and the woman Cleito. Atlas was also a name given to the king of Mauretania in Africa. A fruitful unveiling of mythic realities, even at the cross-over level will help us understand the difficulties of sharing social and intellectual space.

So we also know that Clotho is one of the three fates. She spins and weaves while her sister Lachesis draws out and measures the thread and her sister Atropos cuts and designs the thread of life. Now we know something about the language where the words *atrophy* and *clothes* are common.

But who was Cronos? He was the leader and youngest of the first generation of Titans, the divine descendants of Uranus, the sky, and Gaia, the earth. He overthrew his father and ruled during the mythological Golden Age, until he was overthrown by his own son Zeus and imprisoned in Tartarus. What does the Golden Age have to do with the Time before Time spoken about in ancient Egypt? Why is it that we do not know that Nut, the sky, and Geb, the earth, predate Uranus and Gaia? Whose fault is it that we have forgotten the narratives that build the longest lasting civilization on earth?

To the Greeks, Eros was the god of sexual desire; among the Romans this god was called Cupid. We are all sailing on the sea of Eros who might be considered one of the primordial gods, the son of Aphrodite. A Trojan is a condom and a computer virus, but it is fully in the tradition of Greek mythology to speak of it as a trickster.

Fortūna, the Latin goddess with the Greek equivalent Tyche, was the goddess of fortune and the actual personification of luck. Fortuna is often depicted with a ball or *Rota Fortunae* (wheel of fortune) and a cornucopia (horn of plenty). She might bring good or bad luck and often represents the capriciousness of everyday life.

Hypnos was a primordial deity in Greek mythology, the personification of sleep. He lived in a cave next to his twin brother, Thanatos, in the underworld, without either sun or moon light; the earth in front of the cave was full of poppies and other sleep-inducing plants. Of course, as we know poppies are the source of drugs such as morphine and codeine. When we say Hypnos we are claiming all of the descendants of this very ancient Greek meme. Thus, we say hypnotic, hypnosis, and hypnotize and make these terms a part of our African reality.

Indeed, the ordinary reader living in this environment, especially the European, already has a special advantage in this mythic reality. Think about this mythical idea, in Greek mythology, the root of much of Western memory, Atlas was a Titan who was condemned to hold the world on his shoulders throughout eternity. So it is possible, deep in the crevices of memory, that some Europeans, and now some Africans, believe that European imperialism of the last four hundred years was predicted as the consequence of this Atlasian burden, the white man's burden.

Suppose on the other hand that a mythology is built based on the collective strength of community rather than one individual who becomes an insular hero? What type of people would emerge from such a world? How would a different encounter with reality make for a new people.

CHAPTER ONE

Futures Out of Chaos

Many political, social, and technological changes have occurred since W. E. B. Du Bois anticipated a future that would remake the conditions of African people when he imagined an integrated understanding of reality in the "Comet" published in **Darkwaters**. Yet even today the greatest fear that grips the fascist, strident nationalist, and racist is the knowledge that the deep past of *Homo sapiens* rests in Africa and that many of the elements of the future are in Africa's womb. What is the fear of immigration but the belief that others like us will replace us? At one level it is a cultural fear and at another it is ontological, but it is justified as economic. At the core of irrational racism's hatred is a tightly held existential fear that creates automatic resistance. As Cronus Ampora sings of hope to hold back the forces of the evil magician I am convinced even more now that Africa *woke* with its visions firmly anchored to a speculative future grounded in the virtues of Maat can bring relief. This version of the Afrofuture contains within it the artistic idea of speculative arts, the literary idea of futuristic layers of complexity, and the performative idea of attempting to demonstrate the possible future, for example, in music or dance.

Those nations and peoples who are willing to engage the future will find rewards in **woke** Africa where the consciousness of being is discernible. For example, China has seen the future and it is based in the minerals of Africa. Zambia has seen the future and it is being colonized by China. Airports are being built by China at a fast clip throughout the continent. The small country of Togo has a very functional airport recently erected by the Chinese. I was just there last month. It was beautiful, extremely comfortable, and demonstrated the Chinese mode of hospitality with young beautiful ladies welcoming you to the country holding multicolored pieces of African fabric that were designed in China.

What we wait for is someone to claim that since Cesaire, Senghor, Soyinka, Addo, Achebe, Damas, Diop, Du Bois, Fanon, Ture, Welsing, and Cabral a new cadre of thinkers has been discovered in distant places in our imagination. African Americans are heirs to Rita Dove, Octavia Butler, Audre Lorde, Toni Morrison and Maya Angelou who sat in the high chairs at the table of Richard Wright, Gwendolyn Brooks, James Baldwin, and Ralph Ellison. One can add hundreds of names to a list of outstanding scholars, writers, and intellectuals and never exhaust the depth of African or African American wisdom. There are bulwarks against chaos stationed along the path of our future and those caltrops surrounding our march to a more equitable society have always stopped our enemies from breaking through to utterly destroy our future because we, in each generation, find a source of collective defense against destruction. What are caltrops for our enemies are plinths for us to stand on and proclaim our beingness.

If you do not claim agency you will never create the future; indeed, you will not be in the future. I remember reading the story of a South African demonstration by the AZAPO against a group of whites who had challenged blacks over the killing of animals. It fascinated me because of the culture of death that these whites had presided over during the apartheid regime. Strike Thokoane, the legendary leader of AZAPO, reported that on December 28, 2018 Black protesters ambushed the Clifton beach in Cape Town South Africa and slaughtered a sheep to, cleanse the demon of racism (Azapo Voice, vol 2. No. 1, p. 1).

According to Thokoane white racists were quick to speak about animal cruelty and to act with unity in support of the white residents of Clifton who hired private police to remove Africans from the beach near their houses. The matter was put under investigation by the government because no one came forward to say they had hired the private security company. During apartheid the beaches in South Africa were segregated on the basis of race but black struggle against racism opened them to everyone. The Clifton beaches were among those that were most inaccessible to Black people. Racism undermined every aspect of Black culture including animal sacrifices. Why would whites assume that Africans killing animals to appease spirits were of a different order than they killing animals for sport? They could only arrive at this conclusion because they considered Africans less than whites, of a different order, perhaps even not human as their ancestors had declared in so many ways.

In addition, African religion and languages were considered less than white culture. Whites considered black religion as cults in a negative way while their religion was not cultic, although cultic it actually is. African languages during white occupation were not developed as languages of business, law and science, although they had been prior to the meeting of whites. Africans were not allowed to practice their spirituality which sometimes included the slaughtering of animals. While racists were notorious for perpetuating cruelty against Black people for centuries, they were all of a sudden, activists pretending to protect animals against "cruelty". White racists suggested that Black people had to slaughter the animals in a "non-cruel" way that excludes pain. Shooting the animal was one of the ways proposed by the "know-all and experts" who believed that assassination of the animal with a gun was better than customary rites of the spilling of blood in African traditions. Against this chaos and madness must be the logic of tradition and innovation, not merely the assertion of a white right to command what is best for the customs of Africa. However, I ask, will the African center hold in the future or will chaos engulf us so that we no longer recognize ourselves?

Technically Speaking

There is no "black secret technology" as there is no "white or Asian secret technology"; we are all asserting agencies in an effort to create humans with the modality to listen to many voices and to hear a multiplicity of sounds. There are howeverthousands of mythologies bearing the weight of our future on their imaginative shoulders. One does not see ankhs in hairstyles without recognizing that the ankh is the most famous of all African icons. Like *sankofa* it has become a part of the repertoire of many conscious Africans. Our inclination is to assert what we know and to challenge what we do not know.

Berlin, New York, Paris, Dallas, Shanghai, San Francisco, Cape Town, and Barcelona are the same cities, but we all have different histories underneath the *faux* similarities of buildings, subway systems, parks and stadia; indeed, the new religion is already sport and the stadium in a city is a defining aspect of its contemporary narrative. These new cathedrals of leisure are much like the old ones where people go to watch the sacramental offering of one's self or someone else's self to the cross. In the stadia we see the defeat of our enemies and feel the presence of our own *faux* god.

Reynaldo Anderson in my judgment understands Afrofuturism in its origin more than any one I know. Anderson has been able to trace its origin and to mesh it with his understanding of Afrocentricity as a theory that supports the re-centering of Africans from the marginalities inherent in many European constructions of reality and the future. Like James Stewart, Abdul Alkalimat, and Kodwo Eshun, Anderson has advanced the attachment of technology to the imagination in a chronopolitical and chronohistorical manner. In *Afrofuturism 2.0: The Rise of Astro-Blackness*, Anderson and Charles E. Jones assemble a set of essays that demonstrate the relationship between race and technology and connects, in a powerful reading, the umbilical of Afrocentric thinking, African agency, to the philosophy of the future (Anderson and Jones, 2017).

What this means is that you cannot have a future for Africans if Africans no longer exist. In *Afrofuturism 2.0: The Rise of Astro-Blackness*, he and Charles E. Jones staked out a new periphery in the field of futurism (Anderson and Jones, 2016) and this is the platform from which we have to launch a new orientation to science, art, architecture, dance, and drama (Asante, 2011). One must also add to this discourse the intellectually astute observation of Aaron Smith that what we must do is to introduce an Afrocentric futurism with the substance of a richly complexed African history and Nile Valley sources at the foundation (Smith 2020).

In response to a question about the difference between Black Speculative Arts and Afrofuturism, Anderson said, "The term Black Speculative Arts Movement was coined by the visual artist John Jennings. The movement drew upon previous work by writers, artists, and thinkers such as Sheree Renee Thomas, Tim Fielder, Wanuri

Kahiu, Octavia Butler, Amiri Baraka, Kodwo Eshun, Stacey Robinson, MK Asante, John Akomfrah, and Nnedi Okorafor. I would argue the key event where we acknowledge its existence as a movement was the exhibition *Unveiling Visions: The Alchemy of the Black Imagination* co-curated by John Jennings and me at the Schomburg library in Harlem" (Anderson, 2014).

We are neither relics of race nor endlessly, to use a time frame, dominated people. We are rather a people who has stared down domination time and time again even as we were going to the gallows to be hung by ignorant cowards. Our history is not simply four or five hundred years of resistance to the imperial domination of white racism, which if we speak of relics, is a relic that is still being shelved for a different world. We are and have been free human beings resisting and refusing domination from the very beginning of our encounters with Arabs and Europeans. There never were African slaves; there were only Africans who were enslaved.

Africans are the world and we are the future of this contemporary civilization should it continue without the existential threat posed by ruthless laissez-faire capitalism or ruthless social capitalism. The future may be, despite the wailing wolf of liberalism, a radical social democracy in most of the world. I dare say that there are areas of the world where the lingering illnesses of the colonial inheritances of the past two centuries will have to be stamped out completely by technological transformation. They can no longer hang on to their comfort pillows of racism, sexism, patriarchy, and classism (Stewart. 2004; Nelson, 2002).

I wish I could declare that the multiculturalism of the West and the ethnopluralism of the past are completely bankrupt, but the eruption of Trumpian demagoguery as I have explained in my essay *The American Demagogue: Donald Trump in the American Presidency* convinces me that they are not bankrupt and so long as we declare them vanquished we will not recognize their insidious will to worm their way into our imagination of the future. Therefore, as vigilant as we are in protecting the present, we must be equally attentive to the memes that constitute groundwork for a turbulent future. Racism, anti-Semitism, Homophobia, and Anti-Immigrant reactions are of the same woven fabric that conceals underneath and in the subterranean arena the tattered clothes of impoverished minds.

Vile currents of economic injustice still have the possibility of stealing our future, that is, accelerating the bad tendencies of geo-hegemonic domination that we see in the present. The example of the Congo War, the biggest clash over resources in our generation, is a telling point. In every aspect this war is more prophetic than the Afghan War and the Syrian War or the Saudi-Yemen War because the Congo War is an international war to control the resources of the future. The others are bound up in ideological and religious struggles to control narratives of the past while the Congo War is preeminently about the future.

There is boldness to Reynaldo Anderson's formulation of a radical Afrofuturism that challenges the geo-racial chronus-absorbed legion of devourers of their own children. If a society cannot protect its own children from the monstrous irrationalities of fascism, racism, and masochistic patriarchy it is bound to destroy its own future. Every radical movement must begin with the decisive break with the past and the enthroning of a provocative agency that asserts a firmness that postmodernism rejects. Just as Africans rise from the ashes of 500 years of European colonization and enslavement to define a reality based on the memes of classical Africa we are told that this is a non-condition for postmodernism. Then we must reject this idea that fluidity trumps location from a centered position within a historical narrative. Africans cannot be future oriented if Africans cannot conceive of themselves as subjects and agents responsible for freedom. To be human is to be able to create but this does not constitute *godness* in the sense that one is above others. To be human is goodness enough as the Akan people say in Ghana, that is, to be good is to be human and to be human is to be good.

How will the children know that they are not gods if the fathers falsely promote fratricidal wars where only the survivors operate as tellers of narratives? And if they think they are gods then they are truly being set up for utter death because the future quite certainly will rob them of that delusion.

A question that haunts my own thoughts of the future, especially in the case of African people exerting and asserting agency is "Who speaks for the dead, the glorious dead, whose sacrifices on the altars of manic oppression trails off into faint memories?" Advanced Western civilization as constructed and promoted by demagogues on the false promises of a world freed of people who have color are dangerous ideologies that stunt the ethical, social, and cultural health of any people who propagates them. We have seen it in our own country where the cult of nationalism, literally in Trump's mind, white nationalism, is a phenomenon used for political domination over the masses of people who feel powerless in their own societies. We have seen enough of this on both sides of the Atlantic. We must be done with the Neanderthalian notion of society based on fear, moral weakness, and dishonesty.

Entering a New Future

African people are quickly rejoining a history that has been disjointed, ripped, torn to shreds by the brutal hands of colonialism and enslavement in order to write a future free of fear and threats. We cannot enter the future on the wagons of victimhood, hounded by the dogs of marginality, with our minds centered only on the past; we are not beggar people and out of the thorns and thickets of the past we must pick the fragrant flowers that enlightened and invigorated those futurists who created the cultural, technological and ethical platform upon which we build today.

There is no equal historical time and there will not be any equal future time. As Aunt Aurelia said when in her dementia she had traveled far into the future and had returned to be with me in conversation. "I have been there to see the other side. You know those people over there, you know out there are the same people as the ones who are here. There is bad there and there is good there just like here and now, there is good and there is bad."

Waiting for the future is futile because it will come anyway. When we say "the future" it is almost like we know precisely and exactly when that will be. If we wait for it, when will we see it, and what will it look like if it does not look like us? What is the future if we are not in it? How can we determine what the future will contain? Tim Fielder is an Afrofuturist cartoonist and his works speaks to the fact that we Africans will also be in the future. Without Fielder and Robinson and others who are creating in the context of Afrocentric agency we would wonder what the future would contain.

There are to be sure conditions for transitions; but even then, we cannot be sure that we will be absolutely cognizant of either those conditions or the time of the transition to the future. Just like in the old days and in the present the new society, even the radical Afrofuture, will have the potential for good actions or bad actions. In every case, humans will have to intervene and much of the intervention will be as speculation in the arts, comics, aesthetics, physicality, science, and drone technology just to name a few areas where we will see the changes.

Speculation is different from hope, but it is not prophecy either; it is a focused attempt to qualify and quantify the future based on what we know today. The source of speculation is our current contemplation of the past augmented by our knowledge of mythology, ethics, technology, and aesthetics. I call this necessary combination for speculation *meta* to indicate that it is beyond the theological idea of hope. *Meta* engages us at the individual and collective levels. Individuals are surely agents of change if they are conscious of the *meta* combination. A collective as in a group, community, synagogue, church, mosque, school, club, or corporation may engage *meta* in order to effect change.

One of the burdens of any future, Afrofuture or any other type of future, is the hefty existential question, "Will humans be around to witness the future?" If there are no *Homo sapiens* to witness the future will it exist?

We are confronted with numerous existential threats, some human made and some naturally waiting in the future to intervene in our existence. Science estimates that ninety nine percent of all the species that have lived on the earth since its origin five billion years ago are no longer here. They are gone forever. What gives humans the idea that we will survive and that the future will see us flourish even when the level of risk is greater today than it has ever been on earth? I am not so sure as others are that we will be saved by our inventive technology or our moral compass; it may very well be the cause of our disappearance since humans already have enough nuclear bombs to utterly destroy in the biblical sense every living creature on the earth. Crazy, power driven humans with macho-spirits seeking to test their testosteronic wills may bring us not just to the brink but across the threshold to human elimination as a species.

We live under many threats that we do not think about because thinking about them reduces our chance to experience the possibilities of a future. The earth, our planet, exists in a shooting arena where it is believed gamma rays, at least once, obliterated life on earth 400 million years ago! Who is to say what time it is now? As recent as

2008 there was a burst of gamma rays that hit the earth; such rays can paralyze the entire ecosystem of the earth and bring about an end to everything we know.

Sciencing the Future

Let me cite a few facts that we all know from our general science classes. The universe is estimated to be 15 billion years old. The earth is five billion years old. Hominins started appearing around seven million years ago. *Homo sapiens* first appeared about 300,000 years ago. Our species has not been here a long time and there is no guarantee that we will be here another 300,000 years.

Consider that our entire solar system orbits a black hole 27,000 light years away. Black holes are made by the collapse of stars. If our sun, which is a star, collapses then it would swallow everything; it would be the end of time. Of course, the eventuality of a star collapsing does not have to be our sun; it could be a wandering black hole like the one observed in 2001 moving through the universe as a remnant left over from a super nova. These events are totally unpredictable and do not appear on any human's time scale.

More immediate may be the end of the future from an asteroid like the ten kilometer one that wiped out 65 percent of life 65 million years ago and killed all of the dinosaurs that had lived on the earth for 75 million years. This is precisely why scientists now track asteroids, but a greater danger may even be comets because they are larger than asteroids and travel twice the speed.

As dangerous as threats from space are, they are not the most dangerous, although it is true that they can pose an end to human life. Scientists actually know that some of the most significant threats to the future are home-grown from our own planet. The volcanic threat with danger emerging from the interior of the earth may be the most extreme danger humans face. Volcanoes can appear in many places and we know the visible ones that give us signals of their activities, but a massive volcanic explosion is the one threat that nearly destroyed *Homo sapiens* about 75,000 years ago. The explosion in Sumatra's Mount Toba caused the earth to change and our ancestors in Africa felt the earth grow cooler because it froze at the equator and caused a mighty volcanic ice storm.

Most earth scientists predict that there will be an explosion at Yellowstone, a constantly active volcano, that is 40 miles wide and 80 long, and two miles deep into the earth containing one of the largest magma beds in the world. Like most volcanoes Yellowstone has no predicable cycle but it erupted 600,000 years ago before *Homo sapiens* appeared on the earth.

The future could also be endangered, or at least hostile extraterrestrial forces could endanger *Homo sapiens*. They could come from our solar system or one of the hundred billion stars in our galaxy, the Milky Way, not to speak of others that exist in the universe. Their technologies may be far superior to ours. Of course, if we are the only intelligent life in the universe then there may be no threats, but this is highly unlikely. Such beings if they exist may be extremely hostile and aggressive. I remember reading that large ships of white men approached the Arawak in the Caribbean and three generations later not one Arawak was left.

Perhaps closer to us as threats to our existential reality are microbes, viruses, and bacteria that have proved to be more hostile than any threat so far to humanity. Our scientists are always looking out for pandemics like Ebola, SARS, HIV, and Flu. Humans have not forgotten that flu wiped out 80 million people at the top of the 20th century. The 1918 epidemic killed more people that the First International European War. In fact, it was called the Spanish Flu, and it far exceeded the war's death toll. Flu vaccines have been used to prevent the spread of flu but nothing seems to wipe it out. In fact, viruses abound that can replicate patterns using our own cells. Along with the flu, HIV from monkeys, SARs and Ebola apparently from bats and pets may reform and create retroviruses. As one scientist said a virus can live with us and then appear later and wipe out the entire human race.

Of course, this means that we have to protect ourselves from our own destructive tendencies that have caused humans to create nuclear bombs that have the potential, like nature, to also destroy human future. I visited Hiroshima and went to the museum dedicated to the American attack on Japan and came away shaking with awe at the fact that supposedly reasonable humans went so crazy that they dropped the bomb on Japanese cities. In fact, the Americans intended to drop the bomb originally on seventeen cities, then they reduced it to five, and because of the cloud cover over three of the cities, were only able to strike Hiroshima and Nagasaki. It unleashed a crime of inhuman proportions, it is like the difference between throwing stones and using machine guns.

We Must Not Wait

I think it is essential that Afrofuturists indicate what future we propose and not leave speculation to those who have screwed up the atmosphere, the water, and the soil by advancing predatory capitalist schemes that have changed the climate of the world and endangered our present and our future (Karenga, 2011; Ferreira, 2013). I am not waiting for some mad politician or mad scientist to assume the authority to hold the future hostage. We must all reject the disquiet that can erupt in a world that does not imagine a future because someone or a collective of people seek to steal it. In the United States it is estimated that Donald Trump dismantled nearly 80% of the progressive agenda rules, enacted provisions, and regulations set in motion during Barack Obama's eight-year presidency.

Was this the unbearable truth of a latent racism within the society? (Tal, 1996). Trump's blitz took down laws and regulations protecting health care, water purity, natural habitats for animals, air quality, food production quality, and gun safety. Those who followed him down this path took the ostrich's position despite the inevitability of danger to human beings.

I am pleased by the realization that has come about in the past fifty years that black or African cultural expressions, especially with a strong ethical base as in Charles Fuller's plays about sexual assault in the U.S. military, or Okwui Okpokwasili's emphasis on how the Western world sights African bodies, experiences, contemporary interactions, and futures, and I speculate that these issues and other issues of color, gender, class, and sexual orientation will be rolled into the African political imagination in ways that will produce more Hatshepsutian women leaders in Ethiopia and Liberia, and political cabinets that are fifty percent female in Ethiopia, Rwanda, and South Africa. In a way Okpokwasili has put on stage the black capital that is spoken of in Afrofuture circles.

It is impossible to dream of a future or *the* future without imagination and in so many of us imperial capitalism and centralized statism have murdered the imagination. The trauma brought about by the death of imagination blurs the consciousness of the future and imprisons us in the unacceptable presence where we battle the demons that occupy the highest political, social, and economic spaces. Our materialism has run over to our acceptance of the ownership of all forms of property, even to the creation of other people as property to be owned, controlled, and thrown away when we no longer can find use for them.

Yet we are prepositioned, as any people are positioned, to tackle the cultural, intellectual, gender, and ideological issues of the future (Stewart, 1976, Hendrix et. al, 1984; 2004; Womack 2013; Barr

2008). Our preposition arrives on the backs of our ancestors who squatted in the cotton fields to gain a little rest after hoeing all day. I am child of the hoers who chopped cotton in the thickest jungles of the American south. This was the empire that the whites created in the Americas and the Caribbean. We were and are till this day victims of an economic, political, spiritual, and ethical warfare as pawns in the old cycle of *Homo sapiens-Neanderthalian* antagonisms where the soul of the time, the *geist*, is conflicted with itself because we are all *more* human and less *a-human* as we become more harmonious with each other (Mazama, 2018).

Boaventura de Sousa Santos speaks of the end of the cognitive empire. I am not so sure that we have had a cognitive empire, though it is possible that there have been some political states here and there that have expressed their willingness to be realms of cognition (Sousa Santos, 2018). My fear is that this metaphorical turn of language might encourage the bifurcation inherent in Leopold Senghor's "L'émotion est nègre, la raison est hellène." Sousa Santos sees the end of the cognitive age as bringing into existence the epistemologies of the South. Do we not think? Have we no reason? Is this truly an affirmation of Mazama's European as a-human? This may be Europe's main problem with the future: white thinkers, in America and Europe, maintain the deep categorization of us and them. Even Donald Trump wraps himself up in the theme of his great brainpower. Of course, his irrationality is on display for all to see while his empathy remains in check.

It seems to me that Sousa Santos, whom I like as a person and debated in Chicago several years ago at the American Educational Research Association (AERA) convention, is convinced that Europe has reached a point where there is less efficacy and efficiency in its projection of superior claims. I am certain that numerous authors of the Afrocentric School predicted this fact long ago. I have only to mention Theophile Obenga, Cheikh Anta Diop, and Ana Monteiro Ferreira, Michael Tillotson, Ama Mazama, and Ibram Kendi, for examples (Obenga 20 Diop 1976 Ferreira 2013, Tillotson 2013, Mazama 2003, Kendi 2017). Therefore, Sousa Santos genius comes in pointing to the "south" for possible ways to revive Europe's drive. I am not so sure this is about assisting or strengthening the south but rather about the reinvigorating of the north by appropriating some of the strengths of those who have resisted racism, imperialism, ruthless capitalism, and planned economies with equal fervor.

For me it is victory of sorts to have a European writer admit the failure of Europe to usher in a peace based on justice. There is a bankruptcy in a culture that can only think of, as Michael Tillotson would say, ways of reducing the agency of those considered different by virtue of color, creed, gender or culture. There is however also insatiable greed in the need to rob the South of its resilience against aggression and use that strength to steel Europe against the inevitable attacks on the defining structures of domination.

There is no question in my mind that the blackfellows of Australia have a lot to teach the whites who invaded their land and then claimed that "Australia is a young country" when in fact the blacks have been in that place for 50,000 years. What is it that forces the person who has no shame to summon the will to look truth in the eyes and then to lie with impunity? Are the lies of Trump any different than the lies of the opinion makers, church leaders, corporation elites, and generals, who have lied about the origin of civilization in Australia?

But it is no different than South Africa where the whites made up a narrative of power for occupation of someone else's land by saying that the whites came to the country about the same time as they met the blacks migrating from the north. This was always a lie and it was told with such regularity, written in the texts, preached from the pulpits, that whites believed it and some blacks had begun to believe it before they controlled the government. Now with researchers free to explore and to view the historical realities of South Africa they have had to write a different story. Africans occupied the entire continent for thousands of years before the coming of the whites in the 17th century. In the migration of Africans from the East and Southern Africa why would they leave an entire region untouched in their migration? Why would Africans leave southeast and southern Africa empty of humanity until Jan Van Riebeeck came in 1652?

We are condemned to find our way through the thickets of time to arrive at the meadows of a new future. African nations are entangled in bilateral relationships that deny them the possibility of continental unity. I decry the fact that there is neither a political nor an ideological engine driving the African train; there are only individual and nationalistic desires for advantage often representing precarious ethnic and clan interests instead of a larger, more progressive orientation to society.

If it is true, as I believe it is, that Zambia received billions from China and cannot pay its annual repayment fee then there is trouble looming for the African future, in spite of all progressive advances of Afrofuturism. Why would Zambia make such a deal without some cooperative relationship with another African nation? No small African economic can withstand the power of the United States, China, United Kingdom, or Germany. They are most vulnerable to the assaults on their economies because of the limited nature of their Afrocentric consciousness that what is in the best interest of continental unity is in their best interest. Afrocentricity is a guide for all types of futuristic thinking (King, 1992; Little et.al. 1981)

Imagery is ahead of action because we are stuck with bureaucracies of crass unimaginative types who do not see that actions are possible to make better futures. We call some people visionaries as if they can see farther than others when actually what they are able to do is to overcome the obstacles that confront their imaginations. They have a particular kind of courage that allows them to manifest their images in concrete ways. The founders of giant African industries like Dangote, Adenuga, and Motsepe are called visionaries, but it may be that they had a particularly advantageous perch from which to view the coming era. There are many such stories. I can cite what happened to M. K. O. Abiola or William R. Spivey, two individual Africans who happened to be in the proper place when inquiries about the future came to them and they both responded positively.

Who is to define what imagination is futuristic in African senses? How can we insure that the best Afrofutures are possible? What models do we have in the incubators at this time? What levers of power can be exploited at this time? I have come to believe, in fact, to experience that we create our futures by the very theories that we hold about our social reality. That is precisely why Africa cannot have a future that is African without African assertions, without African agency. Afrocentricity remains the dominant philosophical paradigm to advance the role of African agency urging Africans to interrogate our own histories, experiences, and possibilities (Everett, 2002). I will look only to European and Asian philosophers if I do not know my own. If I know my own, I can also explore others as well, thus giving me a heads-up on what to expect from the futures proposed by others (Asante, 2014). Without that advantage, I am locked in a closet without lights and without a key to open the door to my freedom and I remain unable to assert myself.

It has been observed that whatever theories we have about astronomy they do not affect the stars, the moon, or the planets. However, social scientists often theorize, and their theories become the world we live in. As Afrofuturists we may not have the capacity to affect everything that will happen in the future, but we can, and we do set the platform from which the divers into the deep space of our imagination can leap.

Of course, as we have done in questions of culture, we may have to rethink the idea of ethnofutures or plural futures when we mean Afrofutures, Sinofutures, Gulf futures, etc., while leaving out Europe. I no longer live in a world where Europe is kept out of the circle as if it is above the circle of ethnicities. Europe is itself full of ethnicities. It is like speaking of multiculturalism without including Europeans or it is like speaking of indigenous people without thinking that all people, who are not invaders, are indigenous. As an Afrocentrist I like Europe inside the circle but never above it. I like European cultures to be considered alongside other cultures but never outside of human culture. In the past Europe has put itself outside of human culture by imposing itself as universal. All impositions must be challenged as the first line of ethical value. This is not just a personal cachet but one that is applicable to all forms of bilateral and collective interactions.

Here is the gist of this remark. Afrofuturism removes European patriarchal, masculinist, militaristic, and toxic racism from our future. We urge, of course, our European friends to do the same so that we bring forth into the world a kind of Maatic spirit that pursues peace, harmony, consensus, justice, and reciprocity. What we preserve for the future are the best ideals of ourselves; there is no interest on the part of Afrocentrists or Afrofuturists to preserve into the future the worst examples of our own histories. Like Butler has demonstrated in order for us to face the future we must, of course, turn to the past (Butler, 1979). To be sure there will be clashes, debates, discourse provocations, and ethnic tensions in the future as there are now in the presence because all humans will not be engaged in this process of projected preservation of the best elements. There will be those who will take a Trumpian attitude that they should be only for themselves.

There is real danger that nationalisms can destroy the possibility of cooperative futures. I do not want a racist future of any color and I detest those who seek to intrude into our speculative future with dangerous imaginations of the obliteration of those with whom they disagree. Therefore, I reject all terms of *subalternity, postcolonialism, thirdness*, as Afrocentrists have over the last decades rejected *culturally deprived, underprivileged, minorities*, and *marginality*.

Afrofuturism must mean that people of African descent can project the best ideals and values of a multiplicity of mythological-historical narratives into a speculative space to create a techno-aesthetic ethic based on the best qualities of African people. Such a conception is different from what Mark Dery may have intended in the book he edited *Flame Wars: Discourse of the Cyberculture*. In fact, Dery's "Black to the Future," famously interviewed Sam Delany, Greg Tate, and Tricia Rose, all on the cutting edge of the new black think of the 1990s. For me there can be no Afrofuture without an assertion of African agency, the fundamental element in Afrocentricity. Claiming one's self as an agent of history is the first step to projecting one's self as having something worthy for the future. When Hegel wrote in 1827 that "Africa was no part of history" he was expressing his racism as a part of his concept of Africans as having no agency for historical consciousness.

One of the reasons that Afrocentricity has threatened the patriarchy more than many other ideologies is because it asserts African agency by insisting that there is nothing more critical for African people than their own historical experiences because without those narratives being in the center of our projections, we are nothing more than marginal to other futures. The arrival of the Black Arts Movement in the 1960s until the 1970s was a landmark outgrowth of the

Black Power Movement and the Black is Beautiful campaign. BAM spoke directly to African people, but it did not project a future. One could call it a sort of social modernism or better yet the express and direct artistic and literary response to the African condition as it was in contemporary time. On the other hand, I see Afrofuturism as the artistic, dramatic, performative and literary output of the Afrocentric Movement that is founded upon the idea of projecting African agency into the future. One cannot speak of the future without understanding and appreciating time itself.

On to Time

Time is important because of the cosmic and terrestrial activities that exist within certain chronotopes. Human activity has no impact on the cosmic activities that are constant in the universe. Even if all humans disappear it would mean very little to the cosmos that has been here 15 billion years to our mere 300,000 as *Homo sapiens*. Even the earth, our terra firma, is 5 billion years old and would hardly miss us if we should disappear, perhaps it would revert to a purer atmosphere, with less destruction of the coral reefs, and less melting of the snows at the north and south poles.

Neither terminology nor chronology can be dismissed in the Afrofuture. There is no Trans-Atlantic Slave Trade and there is no Trans-Sahara Slave Trade; there is European Slave Trade and Arab Slave Trade both loaded with historical time and future projections. In the interest of clarity, the platform that we are preparing for a speculative future based on the realities of history must use language that frees us from the past totalitarian constructs of white racial domination. Therefore, I have often warned that Africans can be easily trapped into the language of our captivity. There is no "Black Atlantic" because this trope has neither practical nor philosophical possibilities for our freedom or our future. To divorce Africans living in the United States and the United Kingdom from Africans on the continent is to criminalize families, genealogies, ancestors, and to desacralize our common experiences at the hands of enslavers and colonizers.

Clearly even for me at my age I know that the technical creation of the present with innovations in physics, chemistry, and electronics will produce objects capable of handling space travel and life. We have seen in the film, *Titan*, the imagination of the current humans regarding this situation. A man is processed to live outside of this space and possibly outside of time. Some think it is only a matter of time, not of hardware or software, but of active time, before we are able to advance ourselves. The future envisions not thinking machines but automatons or humanoids that will be hominin in every respect except sexual reproduction. They will of course be programmed to reproduce themselves. All humanoids will disappoint us; they will come looking like us, but they will always be binary creatures. We if we should make it as humanoids into the future will have independent ways of dealing with ambiguity and hypothetical situations.

It is true that when you think that you are describing thought when you are actually describing the processes of selecting and tabulating data you are really silencing thought because selection is not choice in the sense of reasoned thought. Thinking and writing means that you allow something to reveal itself to you after reflection. Now what this means is that we cannot allow ourselves to be deluded by technology or the technical and we should not fool ourselves into believing that we will make the rules for the future.

I fear that our periodization of time is a part of the false history of the world. When we say pre-colonial or post-colonial or pre-modern, modern, and postmodern we are really expressing a political vision that negates African agency and distorts time. I reject terms like *precolonial, post colonial,* and *postmodern* because they are handed to us like universal realities when in fact, they are nothing more than

European particularities. They make no sense to me. One cannot connect one's future to a European universalism that allows neither space nor time for Africa or Asia. We are not merely linked to a dislocation from Europe or an alienation from Europe as if Europe is the central pole; we are disengaged from Africa and that is why we are constantly producing intellectuals such as Paul Gilroy or Stuart Hall or Henry Louis Gates, for example. They are in crisis about the future because they have reached for a Europe that seeks to make them in its own image. Afrocentrists believe it is possible to have many futures and that the legitimacy of the African future is just as valid as any other.

How relevant is a periodization that privileges patriarchy and white racial domination? (Asante, 2007b). Is this something of an obsession of the modern Western world? Do these periods work for Africans and Asians? What is the diachronic understanding of future? What was the language of the future in African languages? As you can see, I have more questions than I have answers.

For Marx prehistory is anything in the West that preceded the socialist revolution that was predicted by him, that is, to say, prophesied. For me there is only gloom and fog before the opening for the revolution and then when Afrocentricity is realized by a critical mass history begins again. Trauma of the imagination is death of dreams and the impossibility of seeing yourself in the future. Imperial capitalism and centralized statism, both destroy the future and hand us the dirty rags of impoverishment of our souls. Our experiences should have prepositioned us for a future bursting with freedom (Conyers and McKnight, 2005).

Afrocentricity seeks to re-center Africans in the midst of our own narratives, not re-write the narratives of Europe or Asia in our image. Only in this re-centering can we best position ourselves to maintain the Maatic balance that will hold back chaos in the world.

References

Alkalimat, A. "Technological Revolution and Prospects for Black Liberation in the 21st Century" Cyrev. URL:http;//www.cyrev.net. (2001)

Anderson, Reynaldo and Charles E. Jones, eds., *Afrofuturism 2.0: The Rise of Astro-Blackness*. New York: Lexington Books, 2017.

Anderson, Sam. "Science, Technology and Black Liberation" *Black Scholar* (March, 1974): 4-18.

Anderson, R., & Jennings, J. "Afrofuturism: The Digital Turn and the Visual Art of Kanye West." In *The Cultural Impact of Kanye West*. Palgrave Macmillan. (2014).

Anderson, Talmadge, and James Benjamin Stewart. *Introduction to African American studies: Transdisciplinary approaches and implications*. Black Classic Press, (2007).

Asante, Molefi Kete. *Afrocentricity: The Theory of Social Change*. Chicago: African American Images, 2011.

Asante, Molefi Kete. *An Afrocentric Manifesto*. Cambridge UK: Polity Books, 2007a.

Asante, Molefi Kete, *Facing South to Africa: Essays Toward an Afrocentric Orientation*. New York: Lexington, 2014.

Asante, Molefi Kete, *The American Demagogue: Donald Trump in the American Presidency*. New York: UWI, 2017.

Asante, Molefi. *The Afrocentric Idea*. Philadelphia: Temple University Press, 1998.

Asante Molefi. *The Painful Demise of Eurocentrism*. Trenton: Africa World Press, 2007b.

AZAPO, Azapo Voice, vol 2. No. 1

Barr, Marlene S. *Afro-future females: Black writers chart science fiction's newest new-wave trajectory*. The Ohio State University Press, (2008).

Bristow Tegan (October 8, 2012) What is Afrofuturism to Africa? http://impakt.nl/archive/2012/essays/tegan-bristow-what-is-afrofuturism-to-africa/ (Accessed November 2, 2015).

Butler, Octavia E. *Kindred*. 1979. Boston: Beacon (1988).

Conyers, James, and Eleanor McKnight. "African-centricity and Techno-scientific Education: A Twenty-First Century Polemic." *The International Journal of Africana Studies: The Journal of the National Council for Black Studies,* Inc (2005): 122.

Dery, Mark. "Black to the Future: Interviews with Samuel R. Delany, Greg Tate, and Tricia Rose." *Flame wars: The discourse of cyberculture*: Durham: Duke University Press, 1994. 179-222.

Eshun, Kodwo. "Further Considerations of Afrofuturism." CR: *The New Centennial Review* 3, no. 2 (2003): 287-302.

Everett, Anna. "The revolution will be digitized: Afrocentricity and the digital public sphere." *Social Text* 20, no. 2 (2002): 125-146.

Ferreira, Ana Monteiro. *The Demise of the Inhuman*. Albany: SUNY Press, 2013.

Hendrix, Melvin, Bracy, James H., Davis, John A., and Herron, Waddel M. "Computers and Black Studies: Toward the Cognitive Revolution" *Journal of Negro Education* 53 (1984): 341-350.

Jackson, Sandra, and Julie E. Moody-Freeman. "The Black Imagination." *Science Fiction, Futurism, and the Speculative*. New York: Peter Lang (2011).

Karenga, Maulana. *Introduction to Black Studies*. Los Angeles: University of Sankore Press, 2011.

King, William M. The Importance of Black Studies for Science and Technology Policy. *Phylon* 49, no. 1/2 (Spring, 1992): 23-32.

Little, William A., Carolyn Leonard, and Edward Crosby. Black studies and Africana studies curriculum model in the United States. *Pamphlet. National Council for Black Studies* (1981).

Mazama, Ama. Ed. *The Afrocentric Paradigm*. Trenton: Africa World Press. 2003.

Mazama, Ama. "The Human and the A-human," lecture at the Molefi Kete Asante Institute, September 2018.

Nelson, Alondra. "Future texts." *Social Text* 20, no. 2 (2002): 1-15.

Okorafor, Nnedi. Who fears death. Vol. 1512. Penguin, (2011).

Sousa Santos, Boaventura. *The End of the Cognitive Empire*. Durham: Duke University Press, 2018.

Smith, Aaron, "Afrocentric Futurism," MKA Lectures, November 15, 2020.

Stewart, James B. "Science, Technology, and Liberation: Foundations for a Black/Africana-Science Technology and Society (STS) Partnership." *In Flight: In Search of Vision*, edited by James B. Stewart, 277-304. Trenton, NJ; Africa World Press, (2004).

Stewart, James B. "Black Studies and Black People in the Future." *Black Books Bulletin* 4, no. 2 (1976): 20-25.

Tal, Kali. "The unbearable Whiteness of being: African American critical theory and cyberculture." *Wired Magazine* 4, no. 10 (1996).

Tillotson, Michael. *Invisible Jim Crow*. Trenton: Africa World Press, 2013.

Womack, Ytasha. *Afrofuturism: the world of Black sci-fi and fantasy culture*. Chicago Review Press, (2013).

CHAPTER TWO

Eshuean Crossroads

This essay dealing with the ideas of Ifeanyi Menkiti and Kwame Gyekye begins with a provocative statement. Most African intellectuals struggle with abandoning Westernity and consequently remain at the Eshuean crossroads.[10] Teasing out our philosophical problems might lead us to a intellectual clarity about the concepts of *community* and *individual* in African cultures. As an Afrocentrist I am eager to know how Africans dealt with thoughts of prolonged existence, knowledge, character, health, and relationships prior to being cast into the world of Western values. Indeed, the question might be, "How Africans carried out the notions of responsibility and regularized the ideas of safety, persons, and community prior to and beyond the cloudiness that came with the Hebraic-Arabo, Greco-Germanic world entanglements?" Of course, here I am using a figure of speech to convey the entire infrastructure of Eurocentric and Arabo-centric consciousness that has warped the minds of our best thinkers.

Eshu is the gatekeeper in Yoruba. Indeed, the names *Elegba, Eshu, Eshu-Elegbara,* and *Legba* represent the appellations by which one considers the active repository of *áshe, esu,* or *asé*. Here in a philosophical sense, it is believed that we can make the implausible plausible, eliminate barriers, guard the crossroads, watch the gates as one passes safely to the other side. It is common to understand an acceptance of the idea that transformation, or in the Kemetic tradition, *khepera,* is truly what happens when we summon *áshe* to ease tensions between the effable and the ineffable and between the crisis of decision and indecision. I have made this gate the entry into the depth of an African quest for discovery.

The reader can understand that we have often been beguiled by the thunder and sky deities who ruled as kings of the gods of Mount Olympus. In one sense Africans have been under this influence since the Arab conquests of the 9th century and the European conquests in the 15th century. We are beholden to all manner of European and Arab gods. Getting the mythologies of whiteness and Europeans out of our minds has been a long-term affair; perhaps it is a semi-permanent condition of the colonized and enslaved until we gain our own consciousness. I am making no attempt to solve this problem in this essay; I simply want to establish the grounds upon which the combatants of philosophical ideas are fighting.

The Pluralism of African Ideas

African ideas are pluralistic, and Africa's people have different philosophies and attitudes toward relationships, societies, culture, and life (Kaphagawani, 1998; Kaphagawani, 2000). We are not all the same has been repeated enough by those who want to emphasize divisions that we must not make the mistake of assuming that the foot fits all sizes of shoes. Furthermore, it is important to recognize the process of interpenetration and intra-penetration of ideas over vast regions of the continent. It is not so much that we are not alone but rather we have not been left alone.

Since one cannot speak for all Africans then we must discover how key writers on any subject have interpreted issues, including the person and community. For example, I must have some idea about the base from which Ifeanyi Menkiti argues a position on community and I must have a similar appreciation for the work of Kwame Gyekye and others on the same or similar subjects. What holds for the term community must also hold for the term individual.

I am first of all inclined to ask, "Is this an African question?" This is always the most important way to deal with any contemporary conundrum surrounding African culture. To know this answer I will have to first examine the principal arguments of Menkiti and Gyekye and then probe them for the most exact pattern of thought. Menkiti's first language is Igbo; Gyekye's is Akan. Yet one should not reduce all African ideas to two or three groups; many African people have dealt with these ideas (Berglund, 1989).

Definitions

The Igbo words for community range from *obodo, umunne,* children of your mother to *umunna,* community or children of the father or *maba,* community. The Igbo word for person is *madu;* however, the word *onye,* can be specific to an individual as one who is destined to be aligned with the deities. Hence the statement that if you agree, your god agrees, shows the deep reflection of a person being related to goodness. You and your god are one. Thus, the Igbo say that the *obi,* the heart, is the center of volition, and can be considered that which makes a person courageous or weak (Emeghara, 1992-1993.)

A good Akan word for community is *abusua,* that is, essentially a group of people who have the same maternal ancestor. The Akan word for person has three components: *okra, sunsum*, and *honam*. Since Gyekye argues that oral traditions are the source of African philosophy it becomes clear that he, much like Menkiti, is seeking to establish the terms of an African response to philosophical issues. Thus, the *okra*, as Kwame Gyekye sees it, must be seen as life force and one can have the life force taken away. The *sunsum* is not physical or mortal and can go and come into the inactive *honam*, which is the physical body, at will. The *sunsum* is where personality, character, and other cognitive aspects of the human being are found (Gyekye,1978).

Postures and Positions

The works of Ifeanyi Menkiti and Kwame Gyekye are keenly important in helping us understand the dimensions of the discourse on community and individuals. These two philosophers have made valuable contributions and although I met both men, I was able to offer Kwame Gyekye a position at Temple and had as high a regard for him as for Menkiti. Both Menkiti and Gyekye represent some of the finest minds of the era. Furthermore they are also excellent writers. Both were trained in philosophy at Harvard, and Gyekye, I know, became an expert on Graeco-Arabo philosophy. While I am not certain what themes attracted Menkiti I know that he has made his history in philosophy on the argument he promoted on the nature of community in African society.

As a poet, with a keen eye toward the metaphor, Menkiti has pushed the line toward the idea of community farther than anyone else and has created more debate around the subject than any other author. I believe however that regardless of Menkiti and Gyekye's contributions and important training in philosophy in Western academies they have found themselves debating something that might not even be an African question but is something similar to "Do Africans believe in polytheism or monotheism?" Here is where you can get a question so far out in space that it has limited resonance with anything African people actually experience. All of this is said to see if I can reframe the "debate" in a way that shapes the discourse toward an African idea remembering always the words of Ptahhotep, one of the most ancient African philosophers who said, "it is good to speak to the future, it shall listen" (Ptahhotep (P) II.42-59, 1956).

Approaching the Subject

We are apt to gain some clarity by beginning at the earliest Kemetic texts. In addition, the body of philosophical traditions that emerge in the orature and literature of spiritual teachings might add to this discourse as well. Others have interrogated these texts long before me and they have been canonized, so to speak, as important enough to be referred to over and over again as significant texts in African thinking. The fact that they are not ordinarily known resides in the same struggle we have had for centuries to overcome the mental oppression brought about by the enslavement and colonization of our people. Appropriation of the earliest African philosophers such as Imhotep, Amenemhat, Amenomope, Duauf, Merikare, and Ptahhotep by a few Western intellectuals has distorted African history (Asante, 2001).

The purposefully mixed philosophical metaphors in the title of this paper indicate the paradigmatic shift that I am proposing in the discourse around the person and community as found in Ifeanyi Menkiti and Kwame Gkekye's dialogue. They are both it seems to me, wrestling with how to best place African people within the constructs of Western philosophical ideas although neither would have agreed to my suggestion that we propose a circle instead of a line because the facility with which we are all captured by the language of the West often constrains us. Rather than a dialogue we are discussing a continuum of possibilities within the framework of the African world. Who would have influenced Africans to consider the individual hero, for instance, in the first place? Where would that idea, the notion of the man alone, or the superhero, come from in African philosophy?

The Yoruba are known to claim that when an infant comes out of the womb he or she is not yet a person; to be a person means that you must be named. One finds that this tradition or custom holds in many other African societies. How is it that Africans in many different places on the continent practice this tradition? The observation that one cannot be considered a person without a name is itself a social observation. You cannot speak, as in English, of a nameless person. Who is that? What is that? A person is a person because a place has been made for him or her within the community according to the tradtion. What exists always is community although the person may or may not exist. One can speak of permanence of community but not of permanence of an individual. But what is a community anyway? Its fundamental quality consists of a lineage. Where do you fit into this lineage?

Certainly, in many African cultures one would not find the idea of an individual over against the community. He who is on the outside of the community is there because he put himself there through shaming the community or violating the acceptable norms. Hence to be an individual is to walk alone; however a person may be alone but has a definite community place.

As generally understood among Africans community does not negate identity as human; it is the gaining of your identity as a person. To be a person is to be human and that is a more robust identification than a singular organism. One can conceivably be an individual without being a person since personhood means that the individual has been accepted as a part of community. Perhaps the interrogation of how individual can exist in the West alone, disembodied from the whole, and insular from all others, will show us how we have been affected by a contrary view that did not exist in the times before Europe or the Arabs. The question that begs to be answered is, "What role did alien religions play in our confusion about the issue of person and community?"

Now lets look more closely at Menkiti and Gyekye in contrast as I have come to believe that they were both deeply influenced by interrogations of European experiences. Yet their positions can be shown to be parts of the same fabric in a circle rather than polar opposites.

Menkiti and Gyekye

Obviously, the question of African philosophy had to be settled in their minds before either Menkiti or Gyekye could respond to the issue of community and person.

Gyekye is quite clear that one does not have to plow the same ground on the question of African philosophy as in the past. He makes a profound observation that "A number of scholars, including philosophers, tend to squirm a little at the mention of "African philosophy," though they do not do so at the mention of African art, music, history, anthropology, religion, etc" (Gyekye, 1984; see also Appiah, 2004).

What we know from the corpus of proverbs is that community appears to be the ideal and the individual is the steppingstone to the ideal. One enters the community as individual not as a community but the nature of individuality is shaped by the prospect of the ideal notion of community. This kind of thinking is difficult for Gyekye who believes that the individual and community should be given equal status. Even given Gyekye's belief I think that one can say the

African perspective rejects categorically the centrality of the individual. Even as we vigorously champion an African individuality as Gyekye does we are bound to accept the ultimate objective of the African philosophical system that claims an increasingly embracing community at this core. Indeed, Emeghara says, "If a neighbour seeks to borrow from you, you give what is needed in confidence. You assist the neighbour who is in trouble without waiting to be invited. The old are respected and cared for as they are the custodians of the societal customs and morality. The older people in the community are regarded as advanced in wisdom and self-discipline. The whole life of a person in the community is geared toward the service of God and humanity" (Emeghara, 1992-1993 p.126-137).

There is an Adinkra symbol "*Woforo dua pa a*" which literally means "It is when you climb a good tree that we push you." This idea captures individual assertiveness and communalism. You must make the decision to climb the tree, but you will make more progress with the community behind you. Julius Nyerere's idea of ujamaa might be said to relate to the notion of communalism that is similar to familyhood.

There are so many proverbs related to group-ness, community, the collective, and togetherness that one cannot deny its importance in African life. Thus, when you remove one broomstick it breaks easily but when you put several together they do not break. Furthermore, the people say, "When two carry, it does not hurt."

Menkiti's Vision

In 1984 when Menkiti wrote "Person and Community in African Traditional Thought" he was already riding the high wave of the rhetoric of African communalism and communitarianism. Although there had rarely been a detailed and structured discussion of the idea that community held primacy over the individual among Africans, it had become the most widely held belief among intellectuals. In fact, William Emmanuel Abraham, also known as Willy Abraham, had written in 1962 a book called *The Mind of Africa* published by the University of Chicago Press that put forth the idea that Africa must be given its space to be itself. As a Pan Africanist Abraham sought to demonstrate the basis for African unity and to show that it could be attained much quicker than the 170 years it took for the American nation to achieve unity. Even with the early work of Abraham on African ways of thinking and Mbiti's *African religions and philosophy* as pillars alongside various anthropological forays into the thickets of African philosophical works it was not until Menkiti's seminal piece that we got a formal discourse on what he conceived as the true position of the ordinary African. After all, the pioneering Kenyan theologian Mbiti was moored into the Christian faith and became one of the leading preachers in Burgdorf, Switzerland. Of course Menkiti was influenced by Mbiti, who was not during that period of time? While some have criticized Menkiti for finding some good in Mbiti's work, others have believed that Mbiti disqualifies Menkiti's work. I do not find this wholesale trashing beneficial because almost all of those who have written after Mbiti have had to deal with the overarching ideas found in his years of fieldwork. What may be more difficult is to answer the question, "Have you not found the true course after all of these years of searching?" Therein is the problem with Mbiti's Christian influence on Menkiti; Mbiti is an unapologetic child of Zeus and his work serves to demonstrate that African ideas are not demonic or anti-Christian religion.

To begin with, Menkiti had to do as all African scholars had to do at this time, that is, to distinguish between African and European ways. It was so easy for Europeans to claim everything that was intellectual or to attempt to put African ideas in a European context so that they could control the understanding of them. I remember, just as an aside, when some European scholars were claiming that Afrocentricity was a variant of European Idealism, not realizing that as a student of ancient African philosophers, including Plotinus, whom some Europeans wanted to give to the Greeks, I did not consider it either a compliment nor something that was correct.

Thus, Menkiti makes the obligatory leaning and argued that Westerners generally held that a person is a lone individual but in African ways of thinking a person is only defined by "reference to the environing community." The fact that Menkiti used a quote from Mbiti to underscore his point seems to lend credence to his idea since John Mbiti's *African Religions and Philosophy* was the reigning tome on the question of what Africans believed at the time. Mbiti had proclaimed "I am because we are, and since we are, therefore I am" (Mbiti, 1970, p. 141). The fact that this is the first quote in Menkiti's article tells us precisely where he is going with the discussion. There is, of course, some reason to believe that Mbiti, as an Anglican priest writing about African religions and philosophy finds his European education a key pivot for an alternative African worldview. Since as we know, the Cartesian idea was "I think therefore I am" it is Mbiti's understanding that African existence was in fact something much more communal. This point does not escape Menkiti who understands that "the reality of the communal world takes precedence over the reality of individual life histories" (p. 171). Interestingly this is something that neither Gyekye nor other critics of Menkiti can successfully argue against. Furthermore, "it is in rootedness in an ongoing human community that an individual comes to see himself as a man, and it is by first knowing this community as a stubborn perduring fact of the psychosocial world that the individual also comes to know himself as a durable, more or less permanent fact, of this world" (p. 171). So Menkiti believes in the priority of the community because to him, as far as he can see, it is ontologically first. One can argue, however, that the single person born into the world comes without community but quickly finds it. What happens for example to the child who is born into the world and then is immediately abandoned by the parents? Menkiti would see this as problematic only because it is untoward in an African sense. Who would abandon a child but an insane person? The communitarian notion, as it is called, depends upon the child being received in community.

Critics of Menkiti have pointed out that there is something "essentialist" in his thinking when he sees a source of community in genealogy, biology, and society. He writes that there is a "mental commonwealth with others whose life histories encompass the past, present and future" (Menkiti, p. 172). Of course, Menkiti was not concerned about literary theories when he presented his argument. I believe that what Menkiti meant is what he revealed in his article that within a certain space and time there are attitudes, behaviors, customs, and legacies that constitute commonalities. Menkiti is not announcing himself as an immutabalist but he is clearly stating the facts of genealogical community. If I am Igbo I am born into an *Umunne* and I become with others the children of my mother.

Now here is the crux of the matter for Africans, one becomes a person because of being a member of community, not because of rationality or will. It is ritual integration that sits at the door of community. You have to become like all of the others who have passed through that door in search of your destiny (Gbadegesin, 2004). There is no mindless notion that this is born in your genes, but there is the common sense idea that when people enter into pacts over long centuries it appears that it is natural to be a part of the existing community. I do not believe that it is natural. I believe that it is something that exists as custom, habit, and tradition. Of course, none of these things is easy to change and why should one want to change them if they work to create character and community. Critics have observed what some problems with Menkiti's formulations. Some have resorted to flighty hyperbole such as saying that Menkiti's views are "as bizarre as they are incoherent." Others have considered the idea of personhood being attained, as in in Menkiti's account, perplexing. Of course, Gyekye has demonstrated his disagreement with Menkiti on the notion of personhood. In his argument Gyekye disputes Menkiti (Gyekye, 1997: 48-49) but I believe that this "dispute" pits extreme views against extreme views and Menkiti is not here to defend himself from the absurdities that surround the pilings on of his work. Gyekye's notion of personhood does permit Menkiti's sense of the evolution of person; it is almost as if Gyekye assumes that personhood is conveyed immediately at birth. One could make that argument but in making it one should be clear that it is aligned to the Western notion of personhood. In Menkiti's world we become, as we grow older and wiser, persons. There is a sense of gaining experience, character, and performing the proper rituals at the root of this idea of personhood. At any rate, it fits perfectly with the ideas known to African societies for years as *khepera*, becoming, noted in the presence of the scarab beetle. Furthermore, the reverence of eldership and ancestor-hood are also connected to this notion that when one is young one does not have the experience to claim the most robust of personhood. Indeed the authentic person is one of the definitive players in the community itself and it becomes eternal as the cycle is repeated forever.

What Menkiti says in quoting the Igbo proverb makes a lot of sense. "What an old man sees sitting down, a young man cannot see standing up."

Using customs to buttress his argument Menkiti says that a child's funeral is not elaborate because the child has not achieved personhood as an old man would have achieved it by the time of his funeral that would be quite elaborate. Clearly in Menkiti's world and that of many other African thinkers the achievement of personhood comes with being accepted into community. If it were simply based on being an individual a child could claim immediate personhood. This is, by the way, not just an Igbo or Yoruba conception, but an idea one finds throughout the African continent. For example, among the Tallensi, according to Meyers Fortes, "No one can be certainly known to have been a full human person until he is shown, at the time of his death, to have been slain by his ancestors and therefore to deserve a proper funeral. This carries the implication that the person thus marked is qualified to join his ancestors and become one of them. So one can say the real test of having achieved personhood is to have had the potentiality, all through life, of becoming a worshipped ancestor or of incorporating one. (Fortes, 1987, p. 257).

Gyekye's View

Kwame Gyekye has argued that one should be careful in treading into the communitarian territory without adequately examining African personhood. He believes that the idea that African personhood is derivative of the community must be thoroughly vetted and discussed in connection with various African ideas. Hence, the arguments made by Kwame Nkrumah, Leopold Senghor, and Julius Nyerere during the era of indepencence and later concretized in the work of Ifeanyi Menkiti may have been overstated. According to Gyekye the African traditional philosophies ascribe value to the individual as a divine being. In his words, the idea that all persons are the children of God means that the idea of individuality does not derive from the community but from the divine. He argues that, in the Akan conception, the soul originates with God. It has an intrinsic value apart from the community in this view. Each person, in Gyekye's view, is conceived as unique, not molded as a uniform copy of others, but as an individual complete so that he or she is not derivative of the community but exists prior to the community. In his view, Gyekye believes that the perons is "ontologically complete" and he quotes the proverb, "when a person descends from heaven, he/she descends into a human society." One cannot survive on his own abilities; that is where the community comes in as a mechanism for person survival. In Gyekye's mind it is an error for the philosopher to think that Africans are only communal. One cannot deny the individual who is a gift of God. There is a theological bent to Gyekye's work that one does not see to the same degree in Menkiti's communitarianism. While Gyekye relies upon Nyame, God, as an intervener at the personal level, that is, the individual comes from God; Menkiti sees the person as having real personality only in the context of the community. Even though Gyekye understands that humans are linked like a chain for him each link is itself separate and individual yet it works in conjunction with the entire chain. To be linked in life and death, then, is to be a part of the communitarian universe with certain attributes that are a part of the whole.

Now let me turn to an attempt to address this situation from an Afrocentrist's perspective where we are interrogating the agency of the subject. I am not so thoroughly convinced as Gyekye that we can divorce the individual from community on the basis of the ideology of a theologically derived notion of descent. The Yoruba philosopher J. Adebowale Atanda claims that the motivating power of Yoruba philosophy is the desire for the good life. One can see this argument in his book, *The Yoruba: History, Culture, and Language*. I would add that the objective of living for most African societies that I have examined can be summarized as: *good character, abundant living*, and *good death*. One cannot achieve any of these objectives without community for it is the community, the family, society, that honors the struggle for good character, rewards abundant living, and declares eternal life as reincarnation.

My claim is that we are persons for sure but we are not truly *authentic* persons until we have claimed and been claimed by community. In our separateness as individuals we are nothing without others who come to mold and shape our characters and announce our entry into abundant life. Shouldn't we want to know what is necessary to achieve the conditions of abundant living? Clearly, African people, in many different ways and across various traditions, have advanced the idea that you must be a good person, even Kwame Gyekye claims so much as this as we shall see, you must have good fortune, and you must have meaningful relationships. Now in Menkiti's world the person does not exist as an infant or young person and does not exist after death; one acquires personhood in the process of working out the relationships with obligations, responsibilities, and community norms and values (Menkiti, 1984). When Jean-Paul Sartre declared that individualism can stipulates unconditioned freedom and choice, Menkiti rejected this notion because his argument is that such unconditioned freedom and choice is not available to every person born into the world. One cannot ignore or abandon the notion of community to arrive at an individualism that is like a lone Iroko tree. Thus, Menkiti would never place a child and an adult on the same level of authenticity. To argue that the community is merely the aggregation of a group of self-interested individuals is anti-African and clearly in opposition to the received wisdom of African societies. Yet as Gyekye realizes we are in a box arguing the issues of person, personhood, individualism, community, and relationships as if these are the terms of African societies.

Let us define the terms that are being used by Menkiti and Gyekye in the best sense as understood by the children of Zeus. Communitarianism relates to cooperative and collectivist communities that give meaning to individuals within the context of traditional values of character, obligations, and relationships. Individualism usually refers to the presence of persons who exist as independent units of free will and choice from birth to death. Thus the debate taken up by Menkiti and Gyekye and numerous other African scholars is one that has roots in the work of Germaine Dieterlen's 1973 *La Notion de personne en Afrique Noire*. Here a European scholar had entered the discourse on what was African by suggesting that the French ethnological tradition had something important to say. Nearly thirteen years later Paul Riesman took on the issue of personhood and individuality in his essay "The Person and the Life Cycle in African Social Life and Thought." Opening up an entire discourse between European writers on who best understood African philosophies of personhood, individuality, and community, the Europeans went so far as to establish the terms of the debate. A symposium at Uppsala in 1987 was entitled "African Folk Models and Their Application" and it addressed the same issues.

Of course, the authors were not content to leave the issues on the table. A book was published and Ivan Karp described the situation as no one but a European writer could say it: "Quite simply, persons sometimes experience themselves in a human way, and sometimes in a Lockean way, and sometimes, as in the case of positivist social scientists, as Kantian transcendentalists. However, these modalities of experience should not be reified and then debated as competing epistemologies. Rather they should be seen as descriptive of the varying ways human beings experience the world according to widely varying needs and interests" ((Jackson and Karp, p. 17). One can see that the work of Menkiti was marginalized in this discourse. Only V. Y. Mudimbe, the Congolese philosopher, sought to bring an African perspective and when one relies on Mudimbe to bring this insight one must be prepared to understand that Mudimbe is also wrapped in the fabrics of Greek and European thinking. Others at the meeting argued that the individual could not be subjective to the community and that the individual had all kinds of power to resist the collectivizing elements and stresses of the community (Jackson and Karp, p. 146). Consequently we have to be grateful for the fact that Menkiti and Gyekye brought the issues of individualism and communitarianism back to a discussion between major African philosophers. This is not to condemn the European initiatives for pushing their own ideas of individuality but rather to compliment the search for harmony in Gyekye and the boldness of Menkiti in stating an African perspective. Gyekye's radical and moderate communitarianism announces his willingness to accept the role of community as advanced by Menkiti without giving up his belief in the individual as a divine entity granted to humans.

The South African philosopher Bernard Matolino's "The (Mal) Function of "it" in Ifeanyi Menkiti's Normative Account of Person" must be seen as a valid critique of Menkiti's normative "it" in reference to the pre-communal and post-communal individual. There is every right reason to argue that Menkiti's argument is informed by Placide Tempels and John Mbiti's views but by the same token clearly the argument that we have had over the issue of African community and individualism is problematic. While I am generally in agreement with Matolino I think he is incorrect to think that Menkiti's views are found in Tempels when in fact they are found in the work of African writers and thinkers prior to Tempels. It is not just Menkiti who argues for the role of personal excellence as dictated by the demands of community; this idea is also found in Gyekye as a part of the Akan philosophy. To say that someone is not a human is to make a moral pronouncement about him as either good or not good. So Menkiti is not far off on this point. When you fulfill the rituals and obligations of the community the more you become a person. One must attain personhood by doing that which is accepted within the community as working to become a good person.

For Gyekye (1997:279), the quality of individuality has two aspects, that of of individual initiative and that of responsibility for one's actions. He believes that in the Akan version of African philosophy this idea of individuality does not lead to selfishness or moral egoism. Although I accept this nuanced notion of individuality I also believe that the profound sense of collectivity as seen in the *Zulu Personal Declaration* has just as much currency in the context of African ways of viewing reality. I quote just a portion of the declaration:

> "I am All-in-One; I am One-in-All.
> I am the circle that encompasses infinity;
> I am the point that is the beginning of the circle;
> I am the value behind the circle" (Asante and Abarry, 1997, p. 373).

It is in this powerful and provocative Zulu declaration that the views of Gyekye and Menkiti find vitality. One says of one's neighbor "He and I are mutually fulfilled when we stand by each other in moments of need. His survival is a precondition of my survival" (Asante and Abarry, 1997, p. 373). Here we see the sparks of individuality within the frame of a collectivity, and this intertwined conception where neither is isolated, best describes the continuum of Gyekye and the realistic presentation of Menkiti. They are, actually, both correct although they have shaded their conclusions with colors mixed from the Eurocentrism of the modern West. In the end the controversy over community and individualism will probably not be resolved in a philosophical manner but rather in a practical demonstration in numerous communities in the African world (Dzobo, 1992).

References

Abraham, Willy. *The Mind of Africa*. Chicago: University of Chicago Press, 1962.

African Studies Quarterly | Volume 12, Issue 4| Fall 2011 http://www.africa.ufl.edu/asq/v12/v12i4a2.pdf

Atanda, J. Adebowale, *Introduction to Yoruba: History*. Ibadan: Ibadan University Press, 1980.

Appiah, K.A. 2004. "Akan and Euro-American Concepts of the Person." In L.M. Brown (ed.), African Philosophy: New and Traditional Perspectives (New York: Oxford University Press): pp. 21-34.

Asante, Molefi Kete 2001. *Egyptian Philosophers: Ancient African Voices from Imhotep to Akhenaten*. Chicago: AA Images.

Asante, Molefi Kete and Abu Abarry, eds., *African Intellectual Heritage*. Philadelphia: Temple University, 1997.

Berglund, A. 1989. *Zulu Thought-patterns and Symbolism*. Bloomington: Indiana University Press.

Dzobo, N.K. 1992. "The Image of Man in Africa." In K. Wiredu and K. Gyekye (eds.), *Person and Community: Ghanaian Philosophical Studies* I (Washington D.C.: The Council for Research in Values and Philosophy): 123-35.

Emeghara, Nkem, 1992-1993. "On the Human Person in African Belief," *Theology Annual*. Vol. 14, p. 126-137.

Fortes, Meyer, *Religion, Morality and the Person*, Cambridge University Press, 1987, p. 257

Gbadegesin, S. 2004. "An Outline of a Theory of Destiny." In L.M. Brown (ed.), *African Philosophy: New and Traditional Perspectives* (New York: Oxford University Press): 51-68.

Gordon, Lewis. *Introduction to Africana Philosophy*. Cambridge: Cambridge University Press, 2008.

Gyekye, K. 1997. *Tradition and Modernity: Philosophical Reflections on the African Experience*. New York: Oxford University Press.

Gyekye, K. 1975: "Philosophical relevance of Akan proverbs" (*Second Order: An African Journal of Philosophy* 4:2, pp. 45–53)

Gyekye, K. 1977: "Akan language and the materialism thesis: a short essay on the relations between philosophy and language" (*Studies in Language* 1:1, pp 237 44)

Gyekye, K. 1978: "Akan concept of a person" (*International Philosophical Quarterly* 18:3, pp. 277–87)

Gyekye, K. 1987: *An Essay on African Philosophical Thought: The Akan Conceptual Scheme* Cambridge: Cambridge University Press; Gyekye, K. 1995: revised edition (Philadelphia: Temple University Press) ISBN 1-56639-380-9

Gyekye, K. 1984 "The Akan Concept of a Person," in Richard A. Wright, ed., *African Philosophy: An Introduction*, University Press of America, 1984. see also Appiah, 2004

Jackson, Michael and Ivan Karp, ed., *Personhood and Agency* (Uppsala Studies). Washington: Smithsonian, 1990.

Kaphagawani, D.N. 1998. "African Conceptions of Personhood and Intellectual Identities." In P.H. Coetzee and A.P.J. Roux (eds.), Philosophy from Africa: A Text with Readings (Johannesburg: International Thomson Publishing Southern Africa (Pty) Ltd): 169-76.

Kaphagawani, D.N. 2000. "Some African Conceptions of Person: A Critique." In I. Karp and D.A. Masolo (eds.), African Philosophy as Cultural Inquiry (Bloomington: Indiana University Press): 66-79.

Matolino, Bernard, "The (Mal) Function of "it" in Ifeanyi Menkiti's Normative Account of Person" *African Studies Quarterly*, Volume 12, Issue 4, Fall 2011.

Mbiti, John S. 1970. *African Religions and Philosophies.* New York : Doubleday and Company, 1970, p. 141

Menkiti, I.A. 1984. "Person and Community in African Traditional Thought." In R.A. Wright (ed.), *African Philosophy: An Introduction* (Lanham: University Press of America): 171-81.

Menkiti, I.A. 2004. "On the Normative Conception of a Person." In K. Wiredu (ed.), A Companion to African Philosophy (Malden: Blackwell Publishers): 324-31.

Onwuanibe, R.C. 1984. "The Human Person and Immortality in Ibo Metaphysics." In R.A. Wright (ed.), *African Philosophy: An Introduction* (Lanham: University Press of America): 183- 97.

Ptahhotep (P) II.42-59, trans. Z. Zaba, *Les Maximes de Ptahhotep*. Prague Academie Ichecoslovaque des sciences, 1956.

Sogolo, G. 1993. *Foundations of African Philosophy: A Definitive Analysis of Conceptual Issues in African Thought*. Ibadan: Ibadan University Press.

Tempels, P. 1959. *Bantu Philosophy*. Paris: Presence Africaine.

Wiredu, K. 1996. *Cultural Universals and Particulars: An African Perspective*. Bloomington: Indiana University Press.

CHAPTER THREE

Understanding a Federal African State: An Historical Example

The United States of America like all governments is a study in contradiction. While it was born with several birth defects including the genocide of the Native Americans and the enslavement of Africans it is thought to have advanced the idea of federalism, the constitutional division of powers between the national and state governments. I say that it is thought to have done this because there is strong evidence that many of the ideas for the United States government came from whites observing the Native Americans, especially the Iroquois Confederation. These people often called the Haudenosaunee, that is, the "People of the Longhouse", are a league of several nations indigenous people of North America. After the Iroquoian-speaking peoples of present day central and upstate New York coalesced as distinct nations, by the 16th century, they formed an association known today as the **Iroquois** "League of Peace and Power".

The original Iroquois League was often known as the Five Nations, as it was composed of the Mohawk, Oneida, Onondaga, Cayuga, and Seneca nations. After the Tuscarora nation joined the League in 1722, the Iroquois became known as the Six Nations. This was fifty-four years before the white Americans declared their independence. The Iroquois Confederacy disembodied in the Grand Council, an assembly of fifty hereditary *sachems* or *sagamores*, paramount kings. When Europeans first arrived in North America, the Haudenosaunee were based in what is now the northeastern United States, primarily in what is referred to today as upstate New York west of the Hudson River and through the Finger Lakes region, and in Quebec, and Ontario. We are still not certain how many of the ideas that we see as emanating from the white American construction are really African. In 1977 the Senegalese thinker Pathé Diagne articulated a thesis that the names of the Native Americans can be correlated to African names and that the characteristics of Native American culture are related to African cultural behaviors. This is incredulous only to those unfamiliar with African traditions and constitutions. Already by the time of the Constitution of the United States of America, Africa had produced various Constitutions of its own, particularly in the Cayor and Songhay empires (Asante 2018). There were, as Cheikh Anta Diop, argues certain constitutional principles that existed by virtue of the traditions of African societies (Diop 1986).

The beginning of the United States of America as we know it coincides with the French Revolution although the United States of America had a first president, John Hanson, who served under the Articles of Confederation. It is necessary to understand that the *Articles of Confederation and Perpetual Union* was an agreement among the 13 founding states that established the United States of America as a confederation of sovereign states and served as its first Constitution. Just as we have sovereign states in Africa, Ghana, Senegal, Benin, Togo, Zimbabwe, and so forth, the states of Virginia, New York, Pennsylvania, Delaware, Maryland and so forth, were sovereign. So when the American states drafted the Articles of Confederation soon after the Declaration of Independence from England, they were placing their feet in the tepid waters of federalism, giving up a little of their sovereignty in order to create a more perfect union of strength. The Continental Congress quickly met in 1776 and created the Articles of Confederation which were then ratified over the next five years by the legislatures of the thirteen independent states. The United States of America under the Constitution did not come into being until the Constitution was signed on March 4, 1789. George Washington became the first president of the United States under the Constitution but during the preceding eight years several other men had governed the union of states.

The process from the Declaring of Independence to formally creating a strong union took thirteen years. We can, if we want to, bring about our "perfect union" in less time than the Americans did in the 18th century. One of the founders of the American nation was James Madison, often called "the Father of the Constitution." It is to him that many people look to for an initial explanation of the idea of federalism as understood in the context of the creation of the government of the United States. Madison explained it this way: "The powers delegated to the federal government are few and defined. Those which are to remain in the state governments are numerous and indefinite. The former will be exercised principally on external objects, such as war, peace, negotiation, and foreign commerce. The powers reserved to the several states will extend to all the objects which, in the ordinary course of affairs, concern the lives, liberties, and properties of the people." Madison sought to separate the federal powers from the states powers; this is the abiding tension in the system. After the election of Barack Obama as president in 2008 many white citizens in all 50 states in the United States signed petitions pleading with the federal government to be able to have a referendum on seceding from the United States. The idea is that states' rights give the people the right to decide if they want to remain in the Union.

Of course, the first time this was attempted, in 1860, it brought about Civil War and 500,000 Americans lost their lives, including many of the 186,000 Africans who fought for freedom. Eleven American states, led by South Carolina and Virginia, sought to break away from the United States and form their own confederacy in order to maintain the enslavement of Africans.

The Union Army, the non-slave states, fought against them and won the victory. From time to time you have a few citizens seeking to exercise their rights to abandon the Union. Most are not considered serious and they will probably never have enough power to overcome the powerful centralized government. While it is a nuisance to the politicians in Washington no one really believes that secession will occur anywhere in the United States of America.

The experience of the Americans with the idea of unity ran into problems under the first attempt under the Articles of Confederation. They found that the states were too powerful and often acted against the interest of the entire nation. Virginia continued to act as if it were not a part of a federal entity, for example, and therefore the weak federal center could not hold. The Constitution Convention held in Philadelphia from May to September 1787 attempted to remedy the system produced by the Articles of Confederation. Under the Articles of Confederation there were several presidents who served for one or two years each between 1776 and 1789. With the Constitution of the United States a strong federal system replaced a weak federal system and created the space for states to exist as equal entities under the federal government.

Thomas Jefferson emphasized the states are not "subordinate" to the national government, but rather the two are "coordinate departments of one simple and integral whole. The one is the domestic, the other the foreign branch of the same government (Bergh 1907)." One of the controversies was whether or not the name should be "These United States of America" or "The United States of America." Over the years the states have merged into "The United States of America." Actually, no other name appears in the Constitution of the United States of America. It has taken time and law to work out the meaning of the union and will take time on the continent of Africa as well. I am certain that some regionalists, nationalists, or localists will seek to retain a sense of autonomy from the union. Events, economic and political, legal and cultural, normally overtake such attempts in a united country.

Opposition

The opponents of the Constitution strongly feared that the states would eventually become subservient to the central government. This is a fear that some African leaders may face even though there would be no reason for any state to fear the central government unless it ventured in the arena of war and peace, commerce, negotiation, and national trade rules and practices. A federal government framework must state clearly what rights the federal government has and what rights are retained by the states. One could see that if you had 55 nations expressing a foreign policy you could create chaos.

Some opponents wondered who would take care of the populations in their states. However, the framers of the constitution claimed that each state would be able to take care of its own people. Madison acknowledged that there was a danger of excessive federal authority but predicted that the states would band together to combat it. "Plans of resistance would be concerted," he said. "One spirit would animate and conduct the whole. The same combinations would result from an apprehension of federal [domination] as was produced by the dread of a foreign yoke; and the same appeal to a trial of force would be made in the one case as was made in the other" (Hamilton, Madison, and Jay 1788). In effect, if Gabon, Senegal, Cote d'Ivoire, Kenya, Malawi, and South Africa refuse in combination to abide by federal edicts or legislation there could be a government crisis. Of course, whatever the issue is enough representatives from these states would be members of the federal legislature so that they could resolve the issue. The early Americans did not want too much government. They believed that the federal government should be limited. They believed (1) that any governmental power threatens individual liberty, and (2) therefore the exercise of governmental power must be curbed, and (3) that to divide governmental power is to restrict it and thus prevent its abuse.

Federalism as a System

Fundamentally, federalism is a system of government in which a Constitution divides the powers of government on a territorial basis. The division is made between a central, or national, government and several regional or local governments. Think back to the Haudenosaunee Confederacy of the Native Americans. Each level of government has its own area of powers. No level, acting alone, can change the basic division of powers the Constitution makes between them. The states cannot on their own seek to end the union. Even the federal government would have to have any amendments approved by the states. Each level operates through its own agencies and acts directly on the people through its own officials and laws.

Division of Powers

The American system of federalism allows local and state governments to make laws about certain things and the national government to make laws about war and peace, commerce, trade, national regulations, and to resolve issues between the states. State laws cannot conflict with federal laws (example: Virginia could not make a law forbidding Africans to vote because the national government has said it is a right for all citizens). Actually, the national government has the power to make laws over a great many issues but the Constitution (10th amendment) says that state and local governments have power to make laws over everything else that the national government does not make laws about. One example is what the federal government says about the voting age. It proclaims that a person has the right to vote at age 18 and it is no different in any state. However, the states have the power to determine the driving speed limit in their state and the national government has no say on what the speed limit should be in Texas or Alaska, or any other state.

What is the Government of the United States of America?

The Government of the United States of America includes a federal government of fifty states, one capitol District of Columbia, and several territories. The federal government is composed of three branches: executive, legislative, and judiciary. The President, the Congress, and the Supreme Court act according to powers in the Constitution and defined by the Congress. There are two houses to the Congress: The House of Representatives and the Senate.

Congress has the power to create lower courts and to create executive offices. Washington is commonly used as a metonym for the entire federal establishment. One can say, well, Washington did not approve, or Washington should make a law and in both cases the idea is the government of the United States of America. Ultimately, it is the states under the Constitution that can give the federal government the right to make laws.

The 10th Amendment to the Constitution is often cited as important in this regard because there are certain things the federal government can do better than states, for example, the printing of currency. Since the state governments cannot print money, they must raise revenue by taxation or

bonds. The budget of states must be balanced and therefore states tend to impose deep budget cuts in times of weak economic growth. Every state has an elected legislature and all with the exception of Nebraska have two houses, bicameralism. Each state maintains its own state court system. In some states, the people elect the supreme and lower court justices; in others, they are appointed, as they are in the federal system. This is really up to the voters of the states.

Challenges of Federalism

What we are seeing more and more in the United States of America is that mobility gives people the right to choose which state they will live in. If one state legalizes marijuana, and another does not then a person will choose where he or she wants to live. If one state takes care of its poor people at a different level than another state then people, as citizens, have a right to move to that state. Some states seek to limit the benefits to their citizens to slow down migration. They offer the fewest rewards, the lowest salaries, and the highest property prices. Some states seek to offer commercial companies the right to operate in their territories without paying high taxes as a way to get their people more jobs. Federalism can create duplication of government administration. If the federal government can operate a program nationally with its workforce why is it necessary for states to duplicate that workforce to carry out the program within their states? Sometimes the states may want to make decisions down to the smallest issue and detail, thus acquiring an expenditure that is unnecessary if the program was coordinated at the federal level.

Some Key Advantages

Without a powerful central government in the United States of America many problems would remain unresolved. For example, the fact that the federal government supported the Civil Rights Movement in the 1950s and 1960s insured the right of Africans to vote although many southern
    states opposed this right. When some states harm others the federal must step in and resolve the issue. Take the issue of environmental regulations. The federal government regulates how much pollution can be put in the air and water by cars and industry. This is necessary because some states would continue to harm their neighbors by polluting the air and the water. Thus, acid rain may be carried from the Midwestern states to the Eastern states and affect the health of people in Philadelphia. Of course, we know that no one in Washington is advocating for protecting the rest of the globe in any strong way although the world is harmed by pollution from the United States. I like the idea of a federal system imposing environmental regulations rather than leaving it to the states. Thus, in Africa there ought to be regulations, at a federal level, for how you mine the land, how you cut the forest, how you kill animals on safari, and how you pollute the rivers, just as starters. I believe that there should be a national policy on education although in the United States of America, the federal government funds education but does

not dictate at the local level what type of education is necessary. I think this is something that an African government would have to revisit in the federal situation set up in the United States of America.

James Madison, in *The Federalist*, argued that the federal system helps prevent factions from gaining too much control and causing tyranny of the majority. Yet we know that states are much more likely to be taken over by factions, ethnic or religious, since they are much smaller than the entire nation. Special interest control of states can be broken by the federal government, as was the case with segregation and racism in the American South. Can you imagine the possibility of the mining interest in Namibia dominating state politics to the extent that it would be against any environmental regulation to protect the health of citizens? Private commercial interests will have to be monitored and a vigilance of government toward corporations will be necessary to protect Africa. In *The Federalist*, No. 51, Madison argued for the separation of powers so as to preserve rights. Yet it seems that it is the states that have more often threaten the rights of the citizens, not the federal government. As people in Africa become more accustom to freedom to explore, create, develop, adventure, and move there will be a desire to protect that form of government.

Onward to the United States of Africa

There will be negative speakers, those who find every reason to insist that a United States of Africa cannot be created. They will cite ethnicity, language, culture, and history and in every case, they will be wrong about the possibilities inherent in the necessary idea of unity. Our committed and patriotic African thinkers have told us that we are more united than we admit; our political philosophers, some that have been politicians, have told us, that with a strong will, and determination we can change forever the character of Africa. A united Africa, operating on a federal basis, can astonish the world with its innovation, power, moral authority, and creative economics. We can do this and nothing should be allowed to deter the African powers from achieving this end. While we were disappointed with the 2007 Accra Meeting, the go-slow meeting as it was called, we know that most of those who were counseling go-slow are no longer in power. They did not act timely and because of that, they will not be remembered in history as bold statesmen and women. However, when we have a cadre of leaders ready to assume the burden of history and place the completion of this dream on the table we will see a burst of Africa glory and pride that will mark the end of one epoch in history and the ushering in of the Age of Africa.

Caution

When Americans established their federal system, the country was. not nearly as it is now. Africans and Native Americans could not vote. Women were denied the vote. The country only had thirteen states and it was eventually to have 50 states. The United States of America would take nearly half of the Mexican nation and annex it to the United States during the 19th century. The states of Maine and Louisiana would eventually express their French Acadian heritage and Florida would turn increasingly Spanish speaking with linguistic, if not ethnic links, to California, New Mexico, Arizona, Colorado, Nevada, and Texas. Africans would become governors of Virginia and Massachusetts and mayors of major cities like New York, Chicago, Washington, Detroit, Atlanta, Houston, Philadelphia, Baltimore, San Francisco, and Los Angeles. Seattle and Portland would express their Japanese and Chinese character in culture and business. The United States would have two Mexican governors in New Mexico, two Hindu Indian governors for two southern states, Louisiana and South Carolina, and several leading Muslim legislators. Of course, whites would remain the dominant political influences into the 21st century and Jews would exercise their power in the legislature, Senate and Congress, as well as being in 2012 the mayors of New York and Los Angeles, the two largest cities in the United States.

Consequently, the earliest founders of the federalism of the United States of America could not predict the future of the country. They could only set the framework and it is that framework that must be set by the leaders of the new African unity agenda. I am an optimist who must say aloud again and again that we need to make this union happen, sooner rather than later, as a measure that will save Africa and bring us the kind of wealth, confidence, union, peace, and happiness that our most revered ancestors have called for during their lifetimes we must declare our will to achieve the United States of Africa. Whether the America example can serve as a model or not, we have on the continent of Africa men and women smart enough, thoughtful enough, and brave enough, to produce the documents, legal and political, that will make a difference in the future of the first continent.

References

Asante, Molefi Kete. *The History of Africa*. 3rd Edition. New York: Routledge, 2018.

Diop, Cheikh Anta. *The Cultural Unity of Africa*. Chicago: Third World Press, 1986.

Hamilton, Alexander, James Madison, and John Jay, *The Federalist Papers* (1788; New York: Mentor Books, 1961), No. 31, No. 39, No. 45, No. 51

Bergh, Albert Ellery, ed., *Letter to Major John Cartwright*, 5 June 1824; in *The Writings of Thomas Jefferson* , ,20 vols. Washington: Thomas Jefferson Memorial Association, 1907, 16:47.

Chapter Four

African Art and Cognitive Narration

All art is derived from the conceptions that we form from our societies. When we are born into a family our first recollections, experiences, sights, and words set in motion our responses to awe. Humans create on the basis of what they have seen and what they come to know. In effect, this process of "coming to know" is what we call philosophy, another way of saying, as the ancient Africans of Egypt said, *sebayet,* the wisdom from experiences. This word, *sebayet,* is where the Greek word *sophia* originates. On the African continent the sages announced our creations and laid the grounds for our artistic structures. Inherent in our philosophies are the necessary conceptions for creating a flourishing future based on the best principles of Maat. According to our classical traditions

Maat was coexistent with the creator. Literally sitting besides Ra as the only other companion in creation.

Background

The earliest examples of philosophy are those that originate on the African continent. There are no philosophers before African philosophers and there are no people who reflected longer and more intensely on the meaning of what was observed in nature and among humans than Africans (Asante, *Egyptian Philosophers*. Chicago: African American Images, 2000).

We are the custodians of a long narrative written and performed by men and women who approached the world with a reverence for and an appreciation of nature. They surveyed the cosmos, explored the bountiful forests, traversed the vast stretches of deserts on the continent, and found the secrets of health and nutrition in the living plants and animals that were here long before humans. They fostered through ritual and ceremony our love for the good and our disgust for the bizarre. In their minds, as in most of our minds, good and beauty amounted to the same thing.

Contours

Early art, as a spearhead of culture, relied upon what was discovered by the scientists and explorers in this continent. Unfortunately the European writers have done us another disservice in a long train of poorly understood ideas and concepts such as the way they have used the terms *hut, primitive, tribes, Black Africa, art* and even the simply term *hunter.*

Much like they have done with other terminology, for example, the difference between *ethnic conflict* and *tribal war* is whether or not it happens in Europe or Africa. By a similar strategy we are confronted with a befuddling of the terms *explorer* or *hunter.* The African is rarely considered an explorer yet that is essentially what the hunter is, one who seeks or searches, by traveling to places other than home. A "hunter" may discover a new village, a people who speak a different language, more productive possibilities for finding meat, a new medicine for a disease, a better route around a mountain, a new process for stalking animals, or a rich area with fertile soil. It was common in the past for these explorers to bring back new objects, precious stones, new animals, and powerfully new stories of what they had seen. They reflected on what they saw and did, and hence became our first scientists. They understood the possibilities of rain or no rain, the sounds of dangerous or harmless animals, and of edible or poisonous plants.

Drawing the Lines

By the time of the 4th Millenium before the Common Era, African classical civilizations had established the rules for art, religion, naming, and writing after a long prologue for history. And during the next millennium would build the pyramids. When Europe says history and pre-history it often leaves the impression that nothing was happening until writing occurred, but alas, Africans had prepared most of the groundwork for human societies long before the appearance of writing in Africa and later in Mesopotamia, today's Iraq.

The universe is nearly 14 billion years old, the earth is barely four and a half billion years old, the dinosaurs after living on the earth for 165 million years disappeared 65 million years ago, modern humans emerged in Africa about 300,000 years ago, and prior to 70,000 years ago most of the time of *homo sapiens*, who were all black, was spent on the African continent.

Before Greece went through one Golden Age the Nile Valley Civilizations, by which I include Kemet, Nubia, Meroe, and Axum, had gone through five Golden Ages. Greece's Golden Age was from 500 to 300 BC. Kemet had gone through the **Inventive Age** where writing, government structures, and ceremony were established from 3400 to 2600 BC; the **Pyramid Age** from 2600 to 2100 BC; the **Restoration Age** of the Middle Kingdom from 2000 to 1600 BC; the **New Kingdom Age** from 1560 to 1069 BC; and the **Piankhian Revolutionary Age** from 746 to 653 BC. Before Imhotep, the black philosopher and architect who is the builder of the first pyramid, called Sakkara, *mr*, in 2600 BC, there are no named philosophers in any other part of the world except Egypt. Our ancestors in Swaziland and in Congo gave us the Lebombo bone and the Ishango bone calculators as the earliest mathematical tools on earth. The Lebombo boneis now said to be more than 44,000 years old and the Ishango bone is 28,000 years old. What are the names of the African women scientists designed the tools to mark the time of their menstrual cycle in such functional manner? Form is often function and both can be decorative.

Africans have never been devoid of art or lacking in imagination based upon our ideas of the cosmos and the meaning of lives in the earthly environment. Each culture has in its own way responded philosophically and artistically to the imperatives of ordinary life. It is true that the mystery of the unknown caused our ancestors to be the first on the earth to name God.

On the African continent the first names of God are recorded as Ra, Amen, Atum, Ptah, and sometimes Khepera.

The Nature of the Beautiful

The first creation story, whether with the Nekhen Theology, Mennefer Theology or the Ionnu Theology, called respectively by the Europeans, Hierankonpolis, Memphis and Heliopolis, was a narrative of cosmic art defining in the first instance the balance and harmony and order that constituted pleasing art. But what did African philosophy say about what was pleasing? In some interesting ways we know so much about what Europe and even the Asians say about art that we have rarely explored our own thinking. The Europeans like to speak about the Golden Mean following the conclusion reached by Vitruv, in the first century BC, that the classical, meaning European ideal of beauty was derived from a symmetry and modular relationship, of the parts, hands and arms and legs, to the whole human trunk on a mathematical basis. They called this the Golden Mean. The Chinese often speak of *Feng Shui*, harmonizing everyone with the surrounding environment, as the keep element in beauty. My old Yoruba great grandfather in Georgia used to say, "Boy, beauty is as beauty does." There is something practical about the African understanding of the cosmic order. It is not better than what the Europeans or the Asians have thought; it is different and difference does not imply ranking as one above another. This is the European falsification of human experiences.

Maat is said to have accompanied the divinity in the creation. One finds in Maat the ideas of justice, righteousness, truth, order, balance, harmony, and reciprocity. This is the most ancient construction of human response to disorder, to chaos, to confusion, and our objective as humans in whatever capacity is to hold back chaos that is the source of evil.

Art is the human production that represents a *re-production* of the divine creation. In a sense, we humans try to imitate nature and thus we impute to the unknown force, that we give metaphorical names to, the idea of creation. Astrophysicists have to see the Big Bang as this initiating force that has created 200 billions of cosmic galaxies.

This is why we claim that humans create art and it is also why the closest we come to divinity is in the act of creativity. In kiSwahili we call this *kuumba*. Sometimes we can say in KiSwahili "alipobuni na kuumba" meaning both the idea of "designed and created." There are few examples of art, whether in the Western classifications that are separate like dance, music, plastic arts, sculpture, or poetry or in the

African unifying concept of art, in kiSwahili, *kuumba,* or ancient ciKam, *Maat.* The completion of this term is important because it is often confused with *sana* which means "very much" as in "*asante sana*" "thank you very much". However, *sanaa* represents completeness in design and quality. One can say, for example, *sanaa bora* or *bora sanaa* to mean something like *good art.*

An Angle

I am a Diopian meaning that I took Cheikh Anta Diop seriously when he declared that African historians must dare to connect African history to its classical origins. Diop said, "The history of black Africa will be written in air until African historians dare to connect it with the history of Egypt." The power of his argument is that Kemet and Nubia are to the rest of Africa as Greece and Rome are to Europe and China and India are to the rest of Asia.

What is the meaning of this for African art and culture? There are three very important aspects of this argument. In the first place, there is an *originality aspect, a justificatory aspect, and an explanatory aspec*t. These are powerful attributes of Diop's understanding of African culture.

Originality Aspect

There are no artistic or cultural elements older than those of classical Africa. This is the originality aspect of art and culture. I have always considered chronology to be a definitive line of thinking in any discussion of the origin of things. A debate over origin can usually be resolved by reference to chronology. Where does this creation fit on the timeline? Am I able to establish a pattern, a texture, a movement, or instrument in the history of African people? I must do this in order to avoid the invasive and assertive false doctrine of African impotence in the face of "outside" influences supposedly arriving from offshore to bring light to Africans in everything from eating utensils to tools for agriculture. Certainly in the minds of the invaders Africans never achieved any artistic competence before the coming of the European.

Colonial Europe made a habit of revising African creations and achievements in a Eurocentric context. Afrocentricity was neither possible nor allowed to be considered at the core of African creative thought. Yet African agency, that is, the creative energy deriving from African responses and understandings of the divine, humanity, and the environment set in motion the cultural revolutions that have produced so much of the world's art. So originality as indicated by chronological methodology allows us to date certain creative achievements that will help us in mapping the future.

Justificatory Aspect

The second element is the justificatory aspect. When one knows one's history it is impossible to be confused. Only those who do not understand the historical record in its actual detail can be lied to, bamboozled, and lead astray.

Remember the mention of Imhotep, probably the greatest human in the ancient world; he was truly unambiguously human, multidimensional, and historic. As I have said in my book, The African Pyramids of Knowledge no ancient figure compares with him in terms of significances to world history and art. He literally guards the gate into the kingdom of knowledge and all of those who think they know something or have walked into the kingdom of knowledge without coming through Imhotep are merely fooling themselves. Homer, the entry point for most Europeans, lived two thousand years after Imhotep.

This vindicatory position that I am calling justificatory aspect means that our connecting all African cultures to the Nile Valley Civilization provides the justification for beginning all our artistic and cultural studies with these early civilizations. I would like to demonstrate historically what I mean by justificatory. I have strictly avoided vindicative because I do not think there is any reason to punish anyone. Vindicatory is, of course, another term for justificatory.

Menes, sometimes called the Scorpion, and sometimes referred to as Narmer or Aha, is the first great conquering king in history. Menes rose in the south of Egypt around 3400 years before the current era and united 42 ethnic communities, *sepats*, along the Nile River and created the world's first nation. In a political sense, then, we know that Menes was a creative political genius. Ruling from Nekhen he commanded a powerful army and organized the religious and spiritual practices that would become traditional among the people of Kemet, the Land of Black People. The Greeks called the land after the temple that they saw, *aigyptos*, meaning "houses of Ptah". Sometimes in the historical record we see the word *Hierakonpolis* and wonder what is its meaning and where is it? This city was called by the Greeks the "City of the Hawks" but the name is derived from Nekhen. The Greeks put their names on many creations that were not there, including cities and towns, concepts and objects. This is like those who called the capital of Zimbabwe by the name Salisbury. The ease with which conquerors wipe out the identity of those who came before is familiar to us today. As it was in the past, so is it often the case now.

So when Imhotep built the Sakkara Pyramid for King Djoser it was the first permanent masonry structure built in the world. No masonry building existed anywhere in the world before this building which I have visited many times. It is a profoundly important structure in Africa that must be seen as the earliest human creation of a temple complex out of stone that remains on earth today.

This opened the pyramid age when peraas Huni and Sneferu build their pyramids and then Khufu, Khafre, and Merikaure had their great pyramids constructed on the Giza plain. More than one hundred pyramids were built in Kemet and more than 200 were built in Nubia.

When the pyramid of Unas, the last peraa of the 5th dynasty, was constructed it contained writing in the interior on the burial chamber which I have seen with my own eyes. It was the first pyramid to have sacred texts written on its wall and on the ceiling.

Thus, the presence of writing at the *nefer isut Unas* "beautiful are the places of Unas" in 2400 BC represents a unique change in way Africans would use sacred writing. It is believed that ciKam, the language of Kemet, arose around 3400 BC, hence, a thousand years later the priests were writing on the walls of the pyramids.

At this point I remind you that Diop's dictum holds and we must re-connect our thinking about art and culture to the classical civilizations of Africa. Over the years I have looked and studied the classical civilizations for every action that is found in other African regions and have been blessed to know how fundamentally concrete and sound our thinking is on the question of African culture. It is essential that you who are the custodians of this massive, complex, and comprehensive gift from the ancestors resurrect its most powerful constituents and put them to use in the African renaissance.

Explanatory Aspect

The third element I have surmised from Diop's comment is the explanatory aspect. All definitions are truly autobiographical and all explanations are either those of your own culture or those of your conquerors. One of the ways that we can access the beautiful as Maat is to know what is the origin, justification, or explanation of a creation. This is apart from the obvious fact that a dance has been created and we call it the *Jeruserema* or a sculptor carves a sacred *hongwe* and we remember where we first saw it. This is the purview of explanation whether descriptive or interpretative. One can know something about a creation by participating in its creation, by studying its use, or by examining its parts.

A rich environment of creation such as we have in the African continent provokes stunning responses and evidences of awe. I was a student at the University of California, Los Angeles during the late 1960s and got into a discussion with the keeper of African art in the Haines Hall basement. He told me that as someone interested in African culture I should see the university's collection. I agreed to go see the collection and I was stunned to see what he said was some of the two thousand pieces of art work that had been taken from the Yoruba people by missionaries who made the argument that the African people should not have these "evil objects" but they were harmless among the whites who understood that they could sell them to universities and museums and make a nice profit on artistic and ritual objects taken freely from Africans who had become Christians. Of course, under the Islamic invasions all of these art forms were under stress to be hidden as in the case of the Cameroonian Tikar or smashed to pieces as in Niger, Mali, and Sudan. The European and the earlier Arab Islamic encroachment on African culture showed little respect for what our ancestors had created. Millions of creations were destroyed systematically in one invasion after another so that they left a stain on our consciousness that something was wrong with what we had created. Waves of studied ways to destroy our creative production left entire stretches of Africa devoid of any real significant objects from the past. This has been the greatest artistic theft in history.

In the minds of the invaders, divinity did not exist among people who had no souls and hence could not be called creators. Everywhere we saw indignities too horrible to describe in relationship to our culture. One does not have to wonder why the degradation of the invaders made such powerful impression on us and even we, the mothers and fathers of human culture, believed what invaders told us.

If they said we had no places of learning, we said, "We have no places of learning." If they said, we had no art of importance, we said, "We have no important art." So this was the way it went in any intellectual or cultural discussion until the rise of Afrocentricity which grounds all African experiences in the agency of Africans. We are the ones who define and determine our destiny. Neither the white god nor the white angels can bring us the salvation we so desperately need in the area of culture. The long history of our dispossession is not a topic for this paper but it has been constant and authoritative.

Finally I would like to propose some avenues for African art that emerge from our history and our observations. In doing this, I am following some of the ideas of Kariamu Welsh who was the first director of Zimbabwe's National Dance Company in 1981. Of course, I have modified her ideas. Now let me suggest that the African idea of reality is permanence of image as rooted in the ancient African idea of eternal life. We were the first to construct the notion of eternal life, *ankh neheh*, and this contrast, for example with the Buddhist notion of *impermanence*, the concept of reality as constant change. In some ways, the African conception may be responsible for the Platonic notions of a realm where the real exists beyond what we see. Plato, after all, studied in Africa. So the idea of flux is not such a major factor in African art although it is becoming more so lately because of intercultural exchanges.

My second observation about art in Africa is that there is little separation between the way we live and the way we create. Indeed in most African traditions we say that there is no such thing as art simply for the sake of art because art is always for the sake of living. How one prepares food, how one pours coffee, who eats first, where does the child sit, who paints the walls of the compound, and so forth? The answers to these questions are found in the fundamental ancestral wisdom handed down for hundreds of years. These answers are in the proverbs. This leads to the necessity for the mature person to master what I call the Seven Systems: Ancestral Reverence, Elder Respect, Proverbs, Dance, Sport, Rituals, Call and Response Singing. Art is closely related to maintaining balance, order, and harmony in society; these are related to Maat and help hold back chaos in the world, hence the eternality of what we do on earth.

In general, ancestral reverence is an essential part of the African conception of family, community, and reality. Elder respect exists as a formative structure for order and it is meant to maintain equilibrium in the society where children who may be clever and imaginative do not overturn wisdom and experience. Proverbs are at the core of one's understanding of how the universe is put together and the wisdom contained in the proverbs comes from nature. Dance and its complement music are bound together in movement representing artistically and functionally the impossibility of finding happiness alone. The person who dances alone is considered strange, perhaps even confused in some cases. Sport is a cooperative venture, something we do for play and fun and competition as demonstration of skills and expertise. Rituals we master in order to insure fertility, the rain, the harvest, the continual flow of the river, and the happiness of our ancestors to keep us safe. The call and response singing is the coming and the going, the giving and the taking, the male and the female. It announces our permanence and demonstrates the dialectic of cooperation as we move to the eternal realm. Welsh says in *The African Aesthetic* that this aesthetic is "visible from popular cultures to classical cultures. In music, dance, theater, film and art, including the body adornment art, there emerge symbols, colors, rhythms, styles and forms that function as artistic instruments and cultural histories" (Welsh-Asante, *The African Aesthetic: Keeper of the Traditions*. Westport, Ct. Greenwood Press, 1993, p. xiv.)

Let me quickly conclude this essay by saying there are many commonalities among people who participate in the African worldvoice. Among these are the following ideas that I call aesthetic traits.

Traits of African Aesthetics

1. Unity of Creation as in Oneness (One piece, the whole, curved lines)
2. Polyrhythmic Waves (Several themes, different sizes, forms, and shapes)
3. Multi-textured Fabrics of Imagination (A Combination of fabrics, smooth and rough, light and dark, humans and animals)
4. Functional Qualities of Manufacturing (Made to be used, in-service, with meaning)
5. Recreation of the Universe (Endless reach for divinity in the creative act)
6. Permanence of Ideal (It can be re-created a thousand times; it is permanent)
7. Festival of Contrastive Color (Strikingly different or even in juxtaposition)

While I am neither a prophet nor a preacher I can see as a cartographer of space might see that African art unrestrained by colonial influences, European domination, or Islamic or other religious prescriptions and boundaries of cultural space might actually add its voice to the chorus of world art in a more vigorous manner than we have seen in the past. Long live African culture and long live the practitioners of this art of permanence.

References

Molefi Kete Asante, *The Egyptian Philosophers*. Chicago: African American Images, 2000.

Kariamu Welsh-Asante, *The African Aesthetic: Keeper of the Traditions*. Westport, Ct. Greenwood Press

Chapter Five

Curricula Insurgency

Hail to the ancestors!
Those who built stone cities and fortresses!
Those who named the forest before Kruger!
Those who called the names of the mountains and rivers!
Those who ventured to every part of this land and wrote their presence thousands of years ago on rocks millions of years old!
Those men and women whose sage voices brought us through the storms of life so that we can be discussing deep questions of our future! Hail to them, all glory to them, may they rest in eternal peace because we will do what we have to do!

The fact is that we have rarely operated on the basis of our own anchoring narratives. Our theories are those borrowed from the newest and most faddish Eurocentric writers.

Today it is Sousa Santos, yesterday it was Marx or Derrida, or someone else whose objective for research and application is tied to a worldview that is not related to the rise of our consciousness. Actually, they neither read us nor cite our intellectuals because they believe in their own superiority. When I was a young professor living in Harare, I had the occasion to listen to the British philosopher A. J. Ayer give an hour speech on philosophy without ever citing a black person. I rose from my seat, surrounded by whites and a sprinkling of blacks, in the university's auditorium and asked the famous philosopher, "Understanding what you have just presented what can you tell us about African philosophy since we are sitting here in Harare?" As whites grew visibly upset, and my black colleagues whom I did not know, seemed agitated that I would question the man, Ayers answered "I know nothing about Africa and philosophy." It was then that I truly understood that although it was only a couple of years after the Second Chimurenga this man had no idea about Africa. He had been one of my heroes as a doctoral student at the University of California because we had to read his book, *Language, Truth and Logic,* that he had written at 27 years of age, in Professor Paul Rosenthal's class. So I eagerly went to hear him at the University of Zimbabwe when I lived in that country as a trainer of journalists for the new government. I was disappointed. Imhotep, Ptahhotep, Merikare,

Amenhotep, son of Hapu, and Duauf are just a few of the Africans philosophers who lived before Thales or Pythagoras or Isocrates, the first Greek philosophers.

I vowed many years ago to break myself from the chains of Eurocentric terms as much as possible to have free rein to reinvent how we deal with our educational needs and possibilities. It has not been bad for me; it has created controversy among those who appreciate my views and those who are challenged by them, but in the end, it matters that we have created a place for Africans to stand that is neither borrowed from Europe nor rented from the Arabs; a place that seeks local capacities for solving local problems in ways that demonstrate our interrelationship to the world.

Afrocentricity is a paradigm; there are many theories that are Afrocentric but the paradigm is what has shifted in the thinking of the most progressively antiracist, anti-colonialist, and pro African intellectuals. I seek that place for our students. In *Afrocentric Manifesto* I established the territory for our inquiry and reasserted Africa's fundamental place in all human narratives and certainly its place in our own histories. We are not junior to any one, and we do not boast about our achievements as if others have not made achievements but no longer can we allow our works and our deeds to be marginalized or swept to the side in the discussion and production of knowledge. Who were the first people to name the days, to make a calendar, to calculate a woman's period?

I am weary of those who believe that African radicalism is only related to economics; they want to claim an African radicalism that relives the Russian Revolution without truly understanding and appreciating the profound value of African Revolution based on rooting out the source of our problems. The aim of any transgressive education, and at this point this is what we must be engaged in, is to disentangle Africans from the subservience that has been fed to us by white overseers. Most African scholars, I include myself, have been taught by white radicals who see the problems of racism, white supremacy, and hegemony that we find in education but they cannot disentangle themselves from their own history. They prefer the role of paternalism, but we have long dispensed with that hierarchical formulation where we were often found going from pillar to post without stopping to interrogate our own ground. Some believed that you had to be either a Marxist or a Capitalist as if the only people who ever thought seriously about how humans live in harmony were Europeans of the last five hundred years. These have been brutal centuries where more than 75% of the native peoples of the Americas were slaughtered, and in some places, a hundred per cent of the people are gone. Africans endured enslavement of the most brutal kind for 246 years in the United States and even longer in Brazil; the aim was to break our bodies and to break our minds. They often accomplished both objectives and we feared that the genocide that befell the native peoples was meant for us. I am here to tell you that we were and we are resilient although we suffer from the same intrusion into our education that you experience. So what we had to say is that as critical as Marxism is of the West it could not produce for us any way forward. I seek a really radical, up from the roots, approach to our situation. The first approach to any Revolution is getting the language correct. Language capture is the most powerful weapon for our liberation.

In education this means a willingness to question everything from the statues on campus to the menu in the cafeteria, from Plato to Marx in an analysis of our situation. Who studies white racism and hegemony? Should not an African university explore how apartheid worked? Would it be useful to examine the source of our deepest problems with education? It is not enough to change the face of the professors, though that is important, but we must change the system that continues to spew out the same rhetoric of negativity when it comes to Africa. Once a system of rewards and punishments based on your relationship to the European ideal is in place it can be carried out by black people against black people. While it is true that liberalism is the most violent system ever known to humans where the Belgians killed half of the people of Congo and the Portuguese, British, French, and Spanish wiped out the people of North and South America and the Caribbean.

A second approach is getting facts straight about knowledge production. The pyramid, the mir, is the fundamental basis for all modern curriculum. It is not found in Greece but in Africa, in Kemet, called Egypt by the Greeks. The pyramid gives us biology, physiology, chemistry, monumental funerals, burial of the dead, and knowledge of the workings of the organs.

A third approach is the decolonizing of the notion of reason. Europe wants to claim reason for itself and to ascribe to other people myths, legends, stories, but not philosophy, not reason. In the mind of Europe the only people who have reason are Europeans. Donald Trump once said that he was really, really smart because he had a German brain and German blood. This is not only silly; it makes no sense and if there are German nationals, they should be ashamed or embarrassed by this type of ignorance. There is no such thing as German blood. As Theophile Obenga has shown, philosophy itself is not Greek, but African because the first people to speak of wisdom, *seba*, were Africans. The word *sophia* is derived from *seba*. This word was first found on the tomb of Antef I around 2120 BC. Greece was not in existence at this time.

I believe that we must ground the next generation of African scholars in Afrocentric thinking, what is in the best interest of Africa is in our best interest.

The Solemn Work of Declining Linkage to a System that Destroys our Children

This may be the most difficult work we will ever undertake; it is more difficult than taking down the political arm of apartheid. The enemy is inside of us and it dominates our thinking so much so that we still pray to a white Jesus and believe that whites have better everything. Some even believe that a white God will greet them at heaven's gate.

There are several propositional regimes that must be challenged: the role of reason as a contribution of Europe to education.

1. The establishment of the Greek –Roman model as the universal model for division of knowledge.
2. The thrusting of Europe's system of hegemonic naming of things as the source of fact.

Actually, for the Afrocentrist any application of a hegemonic model means that there will be insurgency. We know this from historical examples. There are no examples of complete docility of Africans in the face of hegemony. We struggle against all forms of negative assertion, all instances of known threats to our humanity. It was done even when Leopold, King of Belgium, used the evil Henry Stanley to murder and maim the people, we had heroes like Chief Nzanzu of Kasi who led his soldiers against the better equipped *Force Publique* for five years and like Kandolo who defended the wanton murder of the Congolese and mounted a campaign against the Europeans. We know the African American struggle where Nat Turner's men revolted and liberated hundreds from plantations by killing the brutal slave families of Virginia and North Carolina. We know Toussaint L'Ouverture who rallied black people in Haiti against the French colonists and Dessalines who defeated the French Army under the leadership of General Leclerc.

The African story is too amazingly filled with heroes, men and women, who gave their lives for their brothers and sisters to even begin a count, but we must account for their bravery every day as a part of the healing of Zimbabwe.

We know what it takes to have an insurgency against physical violence but we have never practiced our own intellectual insurgency in cases where the enemies of Africa insinuate inferiority, self-defeatism, and ethnic animosities in our minds, All battles begin with ideas, most often bad or false ideas, but they start with someone believing something was said that might not have been said or something that was done that might not have been done. Our system of evaluation must start with the idea that our enemies, those who have consistently undermined us by creating agency reduction formations as Michael Tillotson calls them, must be held accountable for their deeds.

Malcolm X says that the only thing that puts us at a disadvantage is the lack of knowledge of our history. To truly liberate education we will have to liberate our thinkers, our scientists, our religious leaders from the entrapment of whiteness, whether it is the white Jesus or the white Karl Marx. We have among ourselves some of the greatest intellectuals in the world, but you will never be chosen until you choose yourself. So, who controls history? Who theorizes about African history? Why was it not until I wrote *The History of Africa* that a black man had written a continental history? Who has written most African history? Who made the racist J.D. Fage the dean of African history for 50 years? Who has defined our languages as dialects?

Who has called our kings chiefs and their own chiefs kings? Who said that Alexander the Greek was a greater warrior king than Thutmoses III, than Ramses II, than Taharka, than Sundiata, than Hannibal, than Shaka? What we need is an insurgency against racist curricula; we need to debate them and attack them as in a constant state of revolt against our own oppression.

Our Intellectual Oppression

Oppression is not only physical; it is mostly mental. Bobby Wright the great African American psychologist who wrote on the psychopathic white racist mentality said what whites tried to do to us was *menticide*. I was in Australia and saw the treatment of the Native

People of that land by the invaders. It is the same treatment, physical and mental to keep the people subservient. Take away their gods and give them a conquering white god that will now save them. Show me a people's god and I will show you their ancestors or their conquerors.

They told us Africans that we did not have families. The white man said, "I am your father from heaven." They told us we did not have any institutions of higher learning because we did not have their kind of institutions. They told us that we did not have culture just as they were burning our religious relics and ridding us of our inheritances by stealing them and giving them to the British Museum. If you go to the British Museum you leave asking, what did the British ever produce? It is a memorial to colonial thievery. You must wipe the curriculum clean by leading departmental discussions perhaps once a year about how to infuse African content into the curriculum.

For instance, if you are in political science, you want to hold a departmental discussion on what were African contributions to the idea of governing and ruling. Didn't we rule kingdoms, empires, and did not the black king Menes establish the world's first nation in 3200 BC in Africa?

What is extraordinary is that we have not learned our lessons from the experience of colonization of our minds? Why should we honor the racists who have constructed our oppression? The words and works of Thomas Jefferson, Karl Marx, Montesquieu, Goethe, John Locke and hundreds of others must be examined for their ramifications for Africans, not simply as intellectual documents for establishing the European project which is not the same as our project.

I have a friend, let's call him Mutu, who wrote to me and said, "What saddens me the most is to see African or African descent scholars not quoting African scholars who write from an African perspective. They keep quoting the same Europeans, whether they are in the US, Canada, France, Germany, Spain, Portugal, the UK, or the African continent.

I know that we, as Africans, have been removed from our center as you always say and write. A month ago when I introduced myself to a sister from my own country, Gabon, I told her that my first name was Mutu, she said that I was not Gabonese but surely from Congo. When I asked her "why is that?" She said "Mutu is not a Gabonese first name", you're from Congo and have migrated to Gabon". The sister's first name is "Aurelie", which is European! When I said "but what tells me that your "Aurelie" is Gabonese?" Her answer was:"because Aurelie is French and Gabon was colonized by the French!" After her answer, I stopped the discussion and realized how off-centered we still are! We keep seeing ourselves from the colonizers' eyes, despite the horrendous traumas our people have undergone. This sister is not the first one, I've had many times other Gabonese telling me that I'm not Gabonese because of my first name, which is not common, because it doesn't sound French or European!"

Our earliest training used to be the lineages of our families, but the Europeans have trained us away from our own centers, so we know the lineage of Mohammed and of Jesus but have dispensed with our own patrilineal and matrilineal knowledge. What is your name? What is your lineage? Who are your people?

The famous writer Ibram Kendi wrote for the *Journal of Black Studies (Kendi 2018)* an essay entitled "Black Doctoral Studies: The Radically Antiracist Idea of Molefi Kete Asante." Kendi wrote "By founding Black doctoral studies, Asante freed Black Studies in 1988 of the contradiction of depending on scholars trained in historically racist disciplines. This essay reveals the founding racist fathers of the disciplines of sociology, psychology, criminology, geology, geography, political science, history, anthropology, and public health as racists. Almost every discipline in the American academy has been bred in racism. Segregationists expressing Black biological and cultural inferiority founded most of the disciplines in the 19th century and assimilationists expressing cultural inferiority transformed them in the 20th century. But the histories of scientific racism—let alone the disciplines—rarely feature the pioneering scientific racists who birthed and reared disciplines. By hiding this history, the racist origins of these disciplines are buried. In burying the racist origins of these disciplines, we are not able to see Asante's radically antiracist idea: Black doctoral studies" (Kendi 2018).

This is one of the clearest expressions of my intention in creating the doctoral program in Africology and African American Studies at Temple University. This was not a white idea; it was a purely African idea inserted into a white academic structure because I could not find an African institution with the flexibility and confidence to host a truly African school of thought with Family Studies, Engineering and Metallurgy, Agriculture, Ethics and Values, Ancestral Philosophies, Geometry, Orature and Literature, and Music-Dance as fundamental elements of a powerful academy.

Our consciousness has been blurred and we have become drunk with the idea that modernization means westernization.

Four Tactics For Obliteration Of African Consciousness

- **ERASE HISTORICAL MEMORY**/We no longer remember that we are the oldest people on the planet. We no longer remember that Europeans came with an aggressive philosophy to wipe us out.
- **SUPPRESS CULTURAL PRACTICES**/The enemies of Africa always know that culture was essential to people's way of life. If you lose your culture you cannot have a basis for transformation.

- **TEACH WHITE SUPREMACY**/White actors playing imitations of imitations of Africans to delegitimize us/exaggerate of physical features/The teaching of our children that whites can do things that blacks cannot do. The preference for whites in religion, culture, and knowledge.
- **CONTROL SOCIALIZATION AND EDUCATION**/ around the world there is a toothpaste called Darkie. Minimize everything you are, your looks, your hairstyle, your language, your sense of knowledge.

The insurgency must begin at an early age. Now that we know worldwide our populations are placed in disposal positions because we have not been aggressive in our attempt to overcome these tactics it will be up to our youth to destroy these imposed ideas of a mental disorder called racism and white domination, even if no whites are present. Europe could not subjugate Africans without changing us into inferiors; they had to change their way of thinking about Africans. Our children were taught, for example, that ancient Egypt was white, which is false, but which white teachers made many Africans believe.

All white people are not consciously racist; there are some who are designers of racist agendas and others who simply advocate those agendas.

- **Designers**, game maker, created the system
- **Advocate**, buys into system, inherits the system
- Asa Hilliard said some are puppets and others are puppeteers.
- **All disciplines must return to the source and re-Africanize our thinking,**
- **The colonial whites had to destroy group unity and culture.**
- Theology: Africans do not have souls

- Science: Africans are inferior in brain power, *Encyclopedia Brittanica*

The scientists of Europe and the philosophers of Europe created the contexts, the ideologies, the concepts, and the rationalizations for racism against Africans.

We know now that there is a single origin, monogenesis, not polygenesis, of the origin of humanity. All *homo sapiens* derived from Africa, and even the Neanderthals that left Africa and were nearly wiped out by *the homo sapiens* that followed them there, were originally from Africa.

The Keys to Insurgency

1. Tie curriculum to the study of Kemet: first advanced civilization, writing, music, astronomy, politics, philosophy//pre-dynastic and remained the same for 3000 years

Four Golden Ages while
Europe spoke of a mythological golden age.
4241 the calendar was already in place showing that the culture was older than the nation that started in 3400 BC by Menes.

The Golden Ages of Ancient Kemet

1. **Pyramid Age**, 3,4, 5th dynasties, ca. 2700 BCE
2. 11-12th dynasties//**Mentuhotepian Age**
3. 18-19th dynasties//**Thutmoses, Ramses Era**
4. 25th dynasty//**Taharka, Piankhy Nubian Age**

The Greek Golden Age started in the 4th century BCE and ended with the war between Athens and Sparta. Note that this is nore than 2000 years after the first African Golden Age.

Below is a list of the invasions of ancient Kemet by outsiders. These invasions changed the nature of the African country and brought different values, customs, languages, and religions.

Invasions

- Assyrians 627 BC
- Persians 525 BC Cambyses II
- Greeks 333 BC
- Romans 30 BC
- Arabs 631 BC
- Turks 1517
- British. 1799

Egyptologists stole history and bodies of African dead people for their academic study. Tony Browder became the first and most prominent black person to work in archaeology in ancient Kemetic tombs when he joined a team and became a co-leader of the search for Karakhamun's tomb in the Valley of the Kings.

Cheikh Anta Diop showed that the ancient Africans of Egypt were black-skinned people. He measured the skulls and took the measurements of others to show that the people were black. Diop insisted on testing the mummies for melanin, and mummies were tested for bone evidence and many were shown to have African physical structure such as short arms. Furthermore, Kemetic and Nubian figures in tomb of Ramses III, show blood types of mainly type B (whites are mostly A). African scholars have been insisting on DNA studies much like those done on Arsinoe, the sister of Cleopatra, to demonstrate the Africanity of the ancient Egyptians.

All these Greeks said Egyptians were Black

- Herodotus 5th century BC

- Aristotle 4th Century BC
- Lucian 2nd century BC
- Strabo in 1 BC
- Diodorus bc 1 AD

The Bible is not a history book, but we do see this construction regarding the descendants of Ham, one of the sons of Noah, who had these sons: **Kush** *(Nubia-Ethiopia)*, **Punt**, *(Somalia)* **Mizraim** *(Kemet)*, and **Canaan** *(Palestine)*.

Kemet is culturally connected to other Africans.

Kemetiu, the black people with determinative of man, woman.

Of course, we know now that **Ta-Seti**, Nubia, is older than Kemet; Auset and Ausar were in place before the coming of Menes. Primary religion had been done. Heru is already recorded as existing in Nile Valley civilizations in upper Kemet. Also the sciences of Medicine and Astronomy, the language of Kemet (ci-Kam) were thousands of years older than the Christian Holy Family. Kemetic Culture existed almost intact until the arrival of General El As and the Arabs in the 7th century CE who assisted the Africans in removing the Romans but who then took their places becoming the overlords of a black population in 639 CE.

2. Older things are closer to the origins than newer things. Study your own history: review Izalo Y'langa the birthplace of the sun in Mpumalanga, South Africa.

3. We are not spectators//Africans are at the central core of humanity and its civilizations.

4. Each discipline should be reexamined to see if it is on solid foundations of what we already knew before our encounters with Arabs and Europeans.

For example, we know that the Greeks owe their civilization to black Africans! One has to read George G M James, *Stolen Legacy,* and Herodotus' *Histories,* to know these facts that are not widely distributed in the Western Academy. Hence, Philosophy, Astronomy, Medicine, Architecture, Mathematics, and Geometry are all found first in the Nile Valley Civilizations of Africans, not in Europe, America, or Asia.

Among the most famous Greek students of Africa were Homer, Herodotus, Thales, Democritus, Anaximander, Plato, and Pythagoras. It took Martin Bernal's book *Black Athena* to create a debate in the minds of the Europeans. Black scholars had argued these positions long before Bernal, but the interrogation of black scholars was the attempt to say that Diop, ben Jochannon, and John Henrik Clarke had no right to say those things about Greece. In my book, the *Painful Demise of Eurocentrism,* I went through most of the arguments that had been projected by the racists, especially Mary Lefkowitz in her attack tract called *Not Out of Africa.*

Standing at the Acropolis of Athens, one might hear someone say that it all started in Athens. Yet we know that the Parthenon built in the 5th century BCE does not compare in antiquity to the pyramids built around 2600 BCE. The Parthenon is an infant when it comes to construction, even the idea of the columns the Greeks got from Africa.

Democracy, science, and philosophy are not merely Greek; they are stolen ideas from Africa. George James book is called *Stolen Legacy* because he proved that the Greeks got most of their early knowledge from Africans.

5. *Remember to use chronology to prove everything in history. What is Nabta Playa in Nubia? 'What is Adam's Calendar here in South Africa? What were our ancestors doing when Europe was still in darkness?* ***77,000 year old tally instruments in Blombos Cave.***

Who would name the 100,000 to 1 million circles of stones in southern Africa after Adam when they were created tens of thousands of years ago as the oldest known human made objects still standing!

Why is Uluru now called Ayers' Rock in Australia? Who came and changed the names of our ancestral places and made Musi O Tunya Victoria Falls? Not just who dunnit, but why did they do it?

You must practice insurgency. You become a rebel without showing belligerence because it is not about attacking other people; it is simply about righting the wrongs imposed on us by falsifying the production of knowledge.

There are three steps in a mature insurgency.

1. *Deny* all negativity about Africa!
2. *Refuse* to accept language that marginalizes Africans, no primitives, no jungles, no huts, etc. the language must be used to educate, not obfuscate.
3. *Practice* the use of indigenous narratives for examples of science, technology, agriculture, ethics, and social relations. Practice proverbs and sage wisdom as critical thinking. Finally, I have faith in the African scholars of today because I believe with knowledge comes consciousness and with consciousness we will revolutionize the thinking of the youth. *I have faith in the youth. I know you will right the record and advance humanity on the basis of the very values that gave us some of the longest continuous civilizations in the world.*

Reference

Ibram Kendi," Black Doctoral Studies: The Radically Antiracist Idea of Molefi Kete Asante" *JBS,* 49:6, September 2018, pp. 542-558

Chapter Five

In Search of an Afrocentric Historiography

Thanks to the coordinators of the Congress, the Catalan government, members of ARDA, Excellencies, ambassadors, NGOs, and esteemed *amigos* and *amigas* for inviting me to present the inaugural address at this important meeting of scholars and diplomats interested in Africa.

We know that the continent of Africa remains a complex area for scholarly study because the ambiguity of the subject remains a source for imagination, interpretation, and debate. We know, for example, that humans originated in Africa, that it is the most diverse continent in terms of human DNA, that Africa's flora and fauna are among the most extensive on the earth, that it has the world's largest number of languages, that it contains the shortest and the tallest people, and so forth but yet the voice of Africa remains distorted by ambiguity. We do not often hear this voice in history, science, philosophy, and politics because the world creates views of Africa that muffle the voice. Africa's paradox is that it is perhaps the richest continent with the poorest people.

I contend that this is directly related to the fact that for many centuries Africa was forced to speak in the voice of others. My proposal today is to speak about Afrocentricity as a way of approaching African renaissance, to suggest an outline for African historiography, to define Afrocentricity as an advance in discourse about Africa, to discuss the Diopian thesis in regard to this new discourse, to see what some contributions might be, and to end on an optimistic note about the renaissance in African Studies as a precursor to the complete African renaissance. Four weeks ago President Abdoulaye Wade and Foreign Minister Tidiane Gadio of Senegal spoke to a group of scholars about the need for new intellectual ideas for development. The Dakar meeting of December, 2003, will go down as historic for the initiative that was advanced. However, all ideas about renaissance must have substantive theoretical and ideological components.

I developed the concept of Afrocentricity in the late 1970s and early 1980s as an assertion of African agency within the context of Africa's own history, Continental and Diasporan. The issue during the last half of the 20th century seemed to be: "Now that African nations were independent and African peoples throughout the world were gaining freedom from oppression, humiliation, degradation, discrimination, and inequality, what were the missing pages in the book of African redemption?"

It was clear to me at that time that the problem of Africa was not Africa's problem but the problem of Europe's insistence on retaining hegemony over the intellectual and cultural dominion of Africa. Thus, the issue was not merely the political independence of

African nations, the integration of Africans into the body politic of the United States, the creation of new opportunities for Africans in Venezuela, Colombia, Peru, Uruguay, and Brazil, the integration of Africans into European nations, or the end of apartheid in South Africa. These were worthy objectives, based upon struggle and goodwill, and achieved, in some cases, against great political forces.

Yet there remained the problematic of agency, meaning in my view, that what Europe had succeeded in doing to Africa and Africans over the past five hundred years was to remove the normal course of agency, self assertion, cultural definition based on Africa's own historical development, and turning the continent's people and their descendants in other parts of the world into a beggar people. I do not mean this literally but intellectually, which in some senses has literal implications. If I cannot, as a person of African descent, make my own decisions within the context of my own historical experiences then I am forever dependent upon others, who, as it goes, may have been my physical and political oppressors. So to be free from political oppression, free from discrimination, free from the demeaning and humiliating experience of apartheid's social and economic degradation, is only a first step to total liberation which in my judgment comes with being liberated in the mind. Here is the entry of Afrocentricity as a human response to intellectual oppression.

Let me construct the reality of Africa for you so that our discussion of an Afrocentric historiography will have credibility and clarity. When the Portuguese came down the West Coast of Africa in the 15th century they found a land much like that which the Arabs coming across the desert had discovered. It was self reliant, self governing, agriculturally active, and had developed its own systems of commerce and constitutional governance. Ghana itself had arisen in the 3rd Century BC and by the 3rd Century AD had established urban environments at Audoghast and Kumbi Saleh. When

Sundiata Keita defeated the armies of Sumanguru at the battle of Kirina around 1240 African people were still essentially self governing although by this time the influences of Islam had begun to make their marks on the Western Kingdoms as they had in the Eastern region. By the time the Portuguese humiliated King Kwame Ansah and erected Elmina Castle in 1482, six years before Colon arrived in West Africa, and ten years before he landed in Hispaniola, the decline of African independence had become irreversible.

The subsequent tragedies of the European Slave Trade, the Arab Slave Trade, the dismemberment of the continent by the European powers at the Berlin Conference of 1884-1885, and a century of imperial colonial rule on the continent and massive and brutal segregation, discrimination, and apartheid in the Caribbean and the Americas conspired to move Africans completely off of terms: political, economic, social, religious, linguistic, and cultural. There were no African terms respected and honored by the imperial forces of Europe for nearly 500 years. Thus, the colonization of Africa was not only a physical act but an intellectual one. The education of African children in the United States, Jamaica, Martinique, Brazil, the colonies of Guinea-Bissau, Kenya, Southwest Africa, Angola, Equatorial Guinea or Nigeria was similar. The one objective was to create in the African person an individual who was European in thought, education, behavior, attitude, opinions, taste, artistic and otherwise, while remaining black and African only in color. The success of this doctrine is written in the actions and reactions of many Africans from leadership down to the common man and woman who seeks to be European and white as the ideal in life. It is pathetic to see people who pray to a white god, straighten their hair because they are ashamed of their own naturally beautiful hair, and throw parliamentary members outside the chamber because they do not wear

European clothes as they did in Kenya. These are the problems of a culturally, politically, and ideologically confused person.

I argued in my earlier works on Afrocentricity that such a person was dislocated by virtue of being moved off of terms. All reference points for such a person were European. The consequences of such a dislocation were enormous. It meant that those Africans who had been taught in the French schools in Cote D'Ivoire or Guadeloupe that "the Gauls were their ancestors" or the Africans in the United States or Nigeria who had been told that English literature represented the highest form of art in human history or that Africans had no history were being moved farther away from their own agency and being infused, that is, indoctrinated with someone else's story. Now here is the problem with this construction of reality. It is founded upon two insidious and odious ideas, neither of which could be sustained by fair research: (1) Africans are inferior to Europeans, and (2) the only makers of history are European males. We have made progress in putting those ideas to rest. However, there remains much work to be done and many of you sitting in this session have undertaken such work. This is a remarkable achievement against both European and African intransigence in the project to dislocate Africans.

We are able to indict imperial historiography for a large part of this problem, but I am not one to beat a dead horse. I know that scholars have come a long ways from the old days when they argued that Colon "discovered" America or that Mungo Park "discovered" the Niger River. What is not clear, however, to me is that there has been a collective change of heart in the Academy. This will take even more time but it will be done. Of course, I am aware of the work of scholars such as J.M. Blaut whose book *Eight Eurocentric Historians* (London: Guilford Press, 2000) made such an impact a few years ago when he contended that by his reckoning there were four kinds of Eurocentric theory used to explain how Europe grew richer and more powerful than the rest of the world. These were *religion, race, environment*, and *culture*. Of course, according to Blaut, I think prematurely, racism has been rejected and religious explanations are unpopular, and therefore Eurocentrism stands only on culture and environment at the present time. Blaut says "Europe we are told, rose and conquered the world because its environment and its culture are superior: they caused Europe to develop faster and further than every other society" (Blaut, 2000, p. 1). In his judgment this is "false history and bad geography because Europe's environment is not better than the environments of other places—not more fruitful, more comfortable, more suitable for communication and trade, and the rest"(Blaut, 2000, p. 1-2). His thesis is that the rise of Europe is directly related to the year 1492 when Colon's explorations gave Europe a powerful incentive for expansion and conquest.

It is not my intention to take Blaut's position but rather to advance the idea that there are some scholars who are questioning the very bases that served to undermine Africa's own agency and to insert Europe's political and military dominance in the historiography and history of African people. While it is normal for those who take anti-Afrocentric positions to argue against the Diopian or Bernalian theses, few of the same critics have been as severe on the extreme Eurocentric positions that have maintained hostility toward the assertion of Africa within its own history. Both Cheikh Anta Diop and Martin Bernal achieved a good amount of visibility for their bold positions. While both sought to reexamine the manner in wich European scholarship did African history, neither would declare himself an Afrocentrist. In Diop's case the idea had not occurred to him; in Bernal's case the hostility to the idea was not necessary a battle that he had to engage. Yet Afrocentrists have found important aspects of their works to be Afrocentric, that is, they have interrogated African sources for African voices.

Afrocentricity's critics have taken a harsh tone against the idea. The arguments remind me of the grand imperatives of the ancient imperial powers to maintain dependency among the vassals, keep subjects pliant and protected, and to sow discord among the aliens. Like their counterparts in the political and military sectors the academic imperialists, particularly of the 19th century, hold to the idea that no theory could exist if it did not produce dependency upon the extreme European model. This is the crux of the arguments against Afrocentricity and the source of much debate and discourse. My desire is to demonstrate the rational and logical bases of Afrocentricity as a new approach to African reality.

In the first place, Afrocentricity is not a religion and therefore I have never referred to it as *Afrocentrism*. My four books on the subject carry the title, *Afrocentricity (2002), The Afrocentric Idea (1998), Malcolm X as Cultural Hero and Other Afrocentric Essay(1995),* and *Kemet, Afrocentricity and Knowledge*. Indeed, two books by the important Afrocentric scholar, Ama Mazama, have the tittles *The Afrocentric Paradigm(2003)* and *L'Imperatif Afrocentrique(2003)*. It is unclear why those who insist on debating the issue like to speak of Afrocentrism. In English, there is a difference between *Afrocentricity* and *Afrocentrism*. I do not know if this difference holds in Spanish, French, Portuguese, Yoruba, or Kiswahili. The point is that Afrocentricity is not a closed system; it is not a belief system that one has to adhere to in order to reach the kingdom of heaven. As an open system it allows for discussion and debate over the meanings of the key presumptions and assumptions. This is as it should be in any intellectual discourse.

I see Afrocentricity as a paradigmatic quality of thought with implications for analysis and practice where Africans are *subjects* and *agents* of phenomena acting in the context of their own historical *reality*, cultural *image* and human *interest*. Now to claim this definition is not to assail Europe or Asia; it is a statement of African consciousness within the context of historical experiences. The answer to *dislocation* may very well be *relocation* within the center of one's own history. Afrocentricity is **not** the reverse of Eurocentricity as some eager critics have claimed.

It is important to understand the difference as the Afrocentrist sees it. Eurocentricity has become over the centuries an imposition of a particular human experience as if that particularity is universal, thus the imposition has taken the form of ethnocentrism and often racism. Afrocentricity has no part in such a construction and has never claimed a special privilege for Africans on the basis of race, religion, culture, or environment. At one time, Europe spoke of itself as Christendom and when it did, Christendom was seen as being superior to other religious communities. After the battle of Poitiers in 732 when Charles Martel called the members of Christendom together to prevent the Saracens from marching to Tours, Europe discovered itself but, I believe, at that time had not discovered the imperial idea. This would come soon after Colon stepped ashore here in Barcelona to announce his findings and thereby set La Rambla in motion.

Now we come to the true issue. Those who are in power, whether political or intellectual, will do nothing to assist those out of power to throw off their bondage. Any attempt to modify or change the condition of oppression, enslavement, mental or physical, will be met with hostility. The enslaved must exhibit nothing less than total compliance to the will of the enslaver. To raise another possibility, one of freedom of the mind, is to assume that the historically enslaved is capable of making theory, of proposing ideas, of creating new constructs for reflection. I see this problem in the nature of the criticism of Afrocentricity.

It is not possible for me to examine all of the presumptions of Afrocentricity in this essay but I would like to point out some key ideas. One approaches history or any other field, as an Afrocentrist, with the view that there is no anti-place, anti-location or anti-perspective. All issues are richly endowed with location so we argue that the person who claims that European concert music is classical music but Akan court music is exotic "ethnic" music is representing a place, a situation, a location. Just as the person who says classical dance is European ballet, not the dances of the Zulu court or Yoruba traditions, and so forth. Each definer or classifier is making a statement of place. I have been accused of being a perspectivist, but I do not find anything wrong with such designation, and in fact, I rather like the sound of it. Furthermore, I do not know an anti-perspectivist, even my critic is a perspectivist it just depends on which perspective he or she is writing from at the time.

Because Afrocentricity is not a closed system what constitutes African values and ideas are debatable, but they necessarily exist and they are central to Afrocentric inquiry. This also means, contrary to some critics, that the issue of *Africanity* must also be interrogated. What is "African" is as valid to ask as the question, what is "European"? Of course, there are no correct answers to these questions but there are general observations that have a lot to do with historical realities, geographies, and consciousness. I accept, for example, the fact that the white South African or white Australian is more European than their black fellow citizens in those countries. This is not a biologically issue but a cultural practice one, an identification with certain traditions and values that are related to the European experience. Well, in the Americas, in Costa Rica, Honduras, Mexico, Venezuela, Brazil, Cuba, Haiti, Jamaica and other places, there are people of African descent whose histories are parallel to each other and whose cultural practices are related to each other in ways that suggest commonalities. Again this is not biological, but historical, cultural, experiential.

Following the work of Danjuma Modupe, a New York Afrocentrist, who has extended my original formulation, I submit that the minimum characteristics of the Afrocentric historiography project include: (1) an interest in psychological location; (2) a commitment to finding the African subject-place within events and situations; (3) the defense of African cultural elements as we explain and interpret actions and orientations; (4) a commitment to lexical refinement that demonstrates African agency; (5) and a commitment to Afrocentrically, scrutinize data collections in order to revise the collective text of Africans from the standpoint of agency.

In pursuing Afrocentric historiography, we must not confuse *Africanity* with Afrocentricity. Afrocentricity, which is a theoretical perspective, is fundamentally based on a type of consciousness whereas Africanity is simply African people living as African people. I mean the fact that one is born in Africa does not mean that he is Afrocentric since Afrocentricity is a theoretical idea it must be gained by knowledge and consciousness, not by wearing African clothes or speaking an African language. Of course, it is likely that the Afrocentric person will speak a language and wear the clothes, but these factors are not predictors of Afrocentricity.

Afrocentrists make a homological argument that the study of African people from an Afrocentric point of view contributes to the general understanding of humanity. Thus, it is human study that is at the core of our attempt to create a new approach to Africa. We discover Africa's contributions to human civilization by interrogating Africa itself, not by adjusting Africa to Europe's image of it.

Perhaps the most widely discussed issue around the Afrocentric historiography project is the role of Classical African civilizations. Here it is correct to note that most Afrocentrists have taken their cue from the late Senegalese scientist and historian Cheikh Anta Diop, called by African intellectuals, along with W. E. B. DuBois, one of the greatest African thinkers of the 20th century. The publication of his books *The African Origin of Civilization: Myth or Reality* and *Civilization or Barbarism* in 1974 and 1981 respectively, were major English language achievement. Scholars who could not read him in French rushed to purchase his books. Soon Diop was the most talked about black scholar in the United States of America. Led by John Henrik Clarke a chorus of scholars began to sing the name and work of Diop throughout the English speaking world. Everyone knew something about Diop but few had any deep understanding of the tremendous work that he had done. Most of his books and articles remained un-translated from the French. Nevertheless, enough had been done with five of his books in English for Africans in America to characterize him as a major voice in world scholarship. In 1974, Diop joined with the young scholar, Theophile Obenga of the Congo-Brazzaville, to argue the blackness of the ancient Egyptians at the UNESCO Conference on the "Peopling of Egypt" in Cairo. They were overwhelmingly successful in their arguments creating chaos within the ranks of the stereotypical discourse on the nature of Africa and Egypt as a black civilization. In 1986 when he went home to his "village" for his final rest, he had achieved the stature of a modern Imhotep. He had been cited widely, quoted often, and honored in the major academic institutions of the world. His work had received attention belatedly in his own home; nevertheless, his work as the Director of the Radiocarbon Laboratory of the Fundamental Institute of Black Africa soon made him a household name. I should add that he was also a political activist, but, of course, in his research he was strictly a scientist.

What Cheikh Anta Diop did was to construct an approach to African history that unsettled the vast circles of traditional European thought, circles that had included and sad to say, still include, a good number of African scholars. Diop boldly articulated a view, based on extensive research and scholarship in various scientific and linguistic fields that threatened the house of cards that had been erected by hundreds of European scholars in the service of imperial and racial dreams. What was it that Diop said that caused so much reaction? Diop maintained that the ancient Pharaonic Egyptians were black-skinned people with wooly-hair. Why was this a shock to European scholarship? It was the fact that the orthodoxy in Europe had been that the black people had produced no civilization and now Diop is claiming that black people created the most majestic civilization of antiquity. This stunned the established order and caused a sensation throughout the arts and sciences in the universities. What could this possibly mean? If black people are really at the very beginning of human civilization as the mothers and fathers of the monumental civilization of ancient Egypt then what are the implications for arts, culture, sciences?

In 1799 when Napoleon's Grand Army entered Egypt, it took nearly one hundred scholars, people of science and art, along. Under the direction of Dominique Vivant Denon this group later produced the largest book ever written, The Description of Egypt. It immediately caused a sensation in Europe. The drawings, illustrations and commentaries were viewed and read in the leading circles of the European elite. Soon the question was, "Is Egypt a black civilization?" A few writers argued that Egypt was not in Africa, a view that lingers till this day in some of the small hamlets of the American Midwest. Others argued that Egypt was a black civilization but the ancient Egyptians were not blacks. In fact, one argument was that "wooly hair and black skin" did not suffice to say that the Egyptians were black. Of course, here Europe was debating with itself about how to handle the most monumental civilization of antiquity. It was clearly African, but the "black" question was what troubled those who argued for the enslavement of "black" people. If ancient

Egypt is black then geometry, mathematics, politics, sculpture, art, astronomy, medicine, and the names of the gods owe their existence to black people!

Cheikh Anta Diop had started his work on this subject as a doctoral thesis at the Sorbonne to prove that Africa's history had been falsified beginning with the idea that Egypt was not African, indeed, not black. Actually, he was following a long line of writers who had stated that the Egyptians were black. These included Herodotus, Diodorus Siculus, Aristotle, and Count Volney. Furthermore, Diop wanted African scholars to show the connection between ancient Egypt and other African civilizations as a way to gain a new sense of the continental dynamism. In recent times African and other scholars have shown that the interconnectedness of Egypt with other parts of Africa are historical and geographical.

For example, it is now argued by British archaeologists who discovered 30 sites rich in art chiseled into rocks up to 6,000 years ago in the desert east of the Nile River that pre-dynastic Egypt may have had its beginnings in the savannah regions on either side of the Nile Valley. Toby Wilkinson, a Cambridge scholar, who led the Eastern Desert Survey, exclaimed that the rock drawings of cattle, boats, ostriches, giraffes, and hippos suggest that the people who lived in the area in 4000 BC, centuries before the pharaohs or the pyramids, may have been the real source of the Nile Valley inspiration. This type of work is predicted in Diop's analysis and it is my belief that the work of Wilkinson and others serve to demonstrate that Diop had opened up an entirely new vista into the study of ancient Egypt. The people who produced the rock paintings of 4000 BC are similar to the people who produced the older rock art paintings of Africa that go back nearly 50,000 years before the present. One can tell this from the parallel styles of the paintings. Egypt began to turn to desert in about 3,500BC about the time of the conquest of the valley by the southern king, Menes. Before that time, the landscape would have been similar to the present east African savannah with seasonal rivers and waterholes used by animals for drinking. I will not spend additional time on this issue except to say that classical Africa becomes a necessary referent point and resource for Afrocentric concept formation and research and that an adequate understanding of African history, culture, and language cannot take place without reference or responses to classical African cultures.

Thus, Egypt and Nubia are important not simply because of their monumentality but because they predate many of the subsequent civilizations of Africa and one can better understand and appreciate the idea of libation among the Ga by understanding the idea of libation among the ancient Egyptians. Totems are not foreign to classical Africa and our appreciation of totemic developments in other parts of the continent might be enhanced by harking back to the earlier beginnings. Most of all the moral and philosophical concepts such as *maat, maa kheru, iri* and *ankh* are central to explaining much of the African ethical system. Who are Africans anyway? Those who declare themselves as Africans and participate in the same historical consciousness and culture as the majority of the people of Africa must be considered Africans.

Afrocentricity is not data but the approach to data. I do not argue only about the facts of history but also about the approach to the event, situation, or personality. If I cannot find something in a written text I do not dismiss the idea outright because absence of evidence" is not necessarily "evidence of absence." Indeed, there may be a verbal text that is spoken or a text that is written in music. One cannot fabricate or falsify data but one can and should explain as much as possible from the existing elements.

We have, as Afrocentrists, both currency and responsibility. Our currency has allowed us to articulate a new approach to the issues and facts of Africa. It is no longer the study of Africa for the interest of others that motivates us but the study of Africa for itself. In this sense, it is a less selfish pursuit, one based in the clearest desire to see Africa as it, through the eyes of its own people. Basil Davidson, the longtime popular British historian of Africa, once told me that the problem with Europeans is that they cannot get out of their heads this "disbelief" when it comes to African achievements and contributions.

The new historiography is not a false or artificial contrivance. It is a legitimate approach to the place of Africa in the world. It is, therefore, a rational activity dedicated to the understanding of history. What it allows is the explanation of the flow of African history without external mediation. One can no longer speak confidently of Portuguese African history or British African history. One is obligated to write African history with African agency assuming the lead role in the story. And so, we may speak of African resistance to the British, to the Portuguese and to the French. To speak this way is not to deny the agency of the colonialists but rather to assert Africa within the context of its own historical flow. On the other hand, Europe's interventions are minor issues in the long context of Africa. For the European powers, these one hundred or four hundred year involvements can be viewed as ripples in the stream of Europe's own long history. To assert Europe in the midst of Africa is to write over the everyday experiences of the African people. One strikes out the lived histories of the African people by this brazen imposition.

Take the experiences of the various intrepid military, missionary, and merchant Europeans in Africa: Brazza, Mungo Park, Stanley, Livingstone, and so forth. They were not out of Africa's history and experiences, but out of Europe's, as well they should have been. The inspiration, impetus, and ambition which these individuals exhibited were characteristics of the societies that produced them and though they carried out a large part of their activities on the African canvas, the shape of their work was clearly European. For me or you as a scholar to concentrate on what they did as if it were making African history is to promote a narrow, provincial, Eurocentric way of viewing African history.

This is to say that the history of Africa is not based on the actions of David Livingstone in Central Africa but on the actions of the hundreds of thousands of people through whose lands he trespassed. So the Afrocentrist must ask, "Who are these people"? What are their histories? What resistance did they display? How do they see a white man lost in the forest? What do they make of a large train of porters carrying supplies for a white man? Are we able to discover the intimate elements of African history by a close reading of the observations of a European? What special tools are required to evaluate what we read in the journals and diaries of the travelers? Perhaps in the diaries and journals of these merchants and missionaries we are able to discern how the people themselves responded. For example, we know that the name of the grand waterfalls on the Zambezi River was not Victoria Falls before Livingstone but Musi Wa Tunya, that is, the Smoke that Thunders. Yet in the consciousness of Europe and in some Africans it has become, by virtue of Livingstone's arrogance, Victoria Falls. How is this to be understood in African history? What are we to make of this development? I believe a lot depends upon your perspective, the place you take your stand, if you will, *djed..*

The Afrocentrist goes beyond the façade to tease out the agency of Africa. This is not easy but no historiography project is easy. It is a scientific enterprise that requires keen interrogatories just as one would use in examining a witness. In our case the witness may appear to be present but remain silent and we will have to discover our answers in the philosophy, dance, clothing, and material artifacts of the culture.

The battle for truth is tedious. We have often used Greece and Rome as guiding principles in Western Civilization. What would the world have been like had we used Kemet and Nubia as the key classical civilizations? What if Africa itself had been free, unencumbered for the five hundred years that it saw European oppression in its space? What if Africans had been able to use Kemet and Nubia as guiding intellectual and cultural ideas? Would the world be a better place? Would globalization, *mondialization*, be a galloping antelope of Westernization? Would a new ethic of human relations exist based upon the principles of *maat*? One could speculate for days and never come to any conclusive answer about these issues but one thing is certain the missing pages in the book of African redemption are closely related to a new way of looking at African historical data. I have called this Afrocentric historiography, not to be a counterpoint to Eurocentric historiography, but as a statement of Africa's assertion of its agency in Africa's own history.

I am therefore calling for a *constructural adjustment* where Africanist scholars assume a responsibility, regardless of national origin of the scholar, to reassert and re-establish Africa and Africans in the center of their own stories. To me this is the noblest task of the contemporary scholar, one that will have a far-reaching impact on the way we research and study Africa in the years to come. I can see many implications for such an orientation, that is, re-orientation. In the first place, the classical civilizations of Africa will be reconnected to the rest of the continent. Secondly, the emphasis will be more on the moral and ethical content of African societies rather than anthropological studies and methods. This is the point of the work of Maulana Karenga, especially in his book *Maat: The Moral Ideal in Ancient Egypt* (Karenga 2003). Thirdly, there will be a greater appreciation of the relationship between the African Diaspora and the Continent, with more studies on cultural retentions and linguistic influences. I believe that this constructural adjustment will lead us to the renaissance that is necessary in African Studies and will assist in Africa's on charge toward political, cultural, economic, and social renaissance.

Finally, if this renaissance in research is to be done let us be the ones to do it by exploring, for example, the role of Africans in philosophy, gender relations, and family sciences. I am convinced that we cannot understand Africa's contributions to tits own development and the world without examining the basis for society. A list of philosophers such as Imhotep, Ptahhotep, Amenemhat, Merikare, Duauf, Amenhotep, Son of Hapu, Chaminuka, Okomfo Anokye, and others whose thoughts have rarely been exposed should be presented as examples of African achievement. Nubia, from 100 BC to 200 BC gave the world the longest history of women rulers. More than 40 queens ruled in that land, not as wives of kings, but in their own right during a time in which it was difficult for a Roman woman to be called by her own name. What are the implications of Nubia's history for the contemporary discourse on gender relations in Africa and the world? What did Africans do to minimize the creations of orphans and why were there no people without family in traditional Africa? What is the meaning of civilization if it is not what humans try to keep back chaos?

One of the great fields of African inquiry has to be how to maintain justice, order, harmony, balance and peace. Maulana Karenga has shown in his book on Maat: The Moral Idea in Ancient Egypt that this could not be done without truth, righteousness, justice, and reciprocity. I hope today that the *Congreso Internacionale d'Estudis Africans* will join the Afrocentric renaissance and bring into existence a revitalized African studies project.

References

Asante, Molefi. *The Afrocentric Idea.* Revised and Expanded Second Edition ed. Philadelphia: Temple University Press, 1998.

Asante, Molefi Kete. *Afrocentricity: Theory of Social Change.* Revised Second Edition ed. Chicago: African American Images, 2003.

Karenga, Maulana. *Maat: The Moral Ideal of Ancient Egypt.* New York: Routledge, 2003.

Mazama, Ama. Ed. *The Afrocentric Paradigm.* Trenton: Africa World Press. 2003.

Chapter Six

Threats to African Peace

I am neither a diplomat nor the son of a diplomat and whatever knowledge I have about diplomacy I have learned from my friends who are diplomats. I hope that something I say as an activist intellectual with a deep Pan African understanding and commitment will have some influence on deliberations about matters of conflict in Africa.

For me, *conflict is a social, political, physical, or military behavior where one nation or society or group of people stakes out a position that is, or appears to be, incompatible with the position, philosophy, space, or statements of another group and therefore requires extraordinary intervention to resolve the contradictory.* You cannot have the same space that I claim I occupy or vice versa without some intervention whether military or diplomatic. Interventions of the divine are rarely involved in such cases; humans are obligated to work these situations out on their own.

Let me outline a general overview of conflict before I discuss an Afrocentric approach to peaceful solutions.

Types of Conflict

We confront a world of conflict everyday but because human are problem-solving beings the more familiar, personal conflicts are handled in an ordinary, that is, normal course of activities. My brother-in-law wants my mother to stay with him and his family and his siblings are demanding that she be allowed to remain in her own home. My neighbor keeps moving the fence more and more toward my garden and I keep moving it back every time I plant my vegetables. These are typical, perhaps, ordinary arenas of conflicts.

In your home, if a conflict exists over who will eat cold cereal and who will eat oatmeal at the breakfast table, we are likely to move through this without difficulty, so easily in fact that it is not even considered a dispute that had to be settled in order to move on to breakfast. Only when something renders our objective impossible to achieve or obstructs our social interaction do we really have a problem with conflict. It is known that conflict with another person can spoil our day because other people help us define who we are and what are our objectives. Sometimes it appears that conflict does not exist when in fact the appearance is simply a matter of one party, person, society, or cultural group, dominating the other so thoroughly that no voices are raised against the domination. There was a time when whites in the United States felt that there was peace between the races because blacks were so thoroughly dominated by segregation, racism, and second-class status. Conflict becomes overt when a voice is raised against the domination. We see this in many African conflicts.

Of course, some conflicts are not threatening to our person or values; these are nuisance conflicts that can be resolved with a simple agreement between the parties involved. Unfortunately we live in a world where conflicts are not always so easily resolved and solutions are dependent upon understanding and utilizing higher skills of conflict resolution.

There are many types of conflict. Some conflicts appear intractable, but of course, all conflicts have beginnings and will have ends. We can manage conflict easier than we can resolve conflict.

But conflict management is not the same as conflict resolution. Since we are confronted with conflict as a part of the current African reality, it is important that we remember the anonymous Peul proverb that says, "the more you engage in conflict, the more likely someone will suffer."

Four Major Types of Conflict

Four major types of conflict plague Africa: *Fact conflicts, Interest conflicts, value conflicts,* and *structural conflicts*. Accordingly, each type of conflict has its own special characteristics.

Fact conflicts are over misunderstandings or miscommunications about a particular set of information. It is when two parties hold different views about what was said at a meeting, what was meant by a particular international action, or who actually represented what was told to another body. There are often historical or traditional narratives that accompany conflicts of fact. Let us look at a few examples.

Sudan and South Sudan: Sudan's independence was preceded by two civil wars, from 1955 to 1972 and from 1983 to 2005, in which 2.5 million people were killed and more than 5 million externally displaced. Relations between the two states have been marked by several conflicts, including those over the Greater Nile Oil Pipeline and the disputed regions of Abyei and Heglig. In January 2012, South Sudan shut down all of its oil fields in a dispute over the fees Sudan demanded to transit oil. Debates about the nature of this conflict often constitute misinformation, miscalculations, and attempts to seize advantage.

In May 2011 the government of Sudan seized control of Abyei, a disputed oil-rich border region, with a force of approximately 5,000 soldiers after three days of clashes with South Sudanese forces. Abyei represented a fact conflict although the dispute had a serious historical and traditional reality other than the immediate dispute as to who owned Abyei. After the shelling of South Sudan by the Khartoum government, the people in Juba declared that Sudan had committed an act of war. The United Nations dispatched an envoy to Khartoum. Ultimately South Sudan withdrew its military forces from Abyei. The United Nations Interim Security Force for Abyei, consisting of Ethiopian troops was deployed under a UNSC resolution of June 27, 2011. Heglig, another town in the south of Sudan, and Abyei are still disputed despite the actions taken in 2012.

Interest conflicts occur when two or more nations desire the same position, prestige object such as oil fields or mineral regions, or special relationships to trading partners, and so forth. Thus they find themselves competing over the same material interests that might be related to the future growth of a region or country. Let us example in a limited way one aspect of the situation in the Democratic Republic of Congo.

The Democratic Republic of Congo Conflict: The Congo Cauldron of War alarmed the whole of Africa and claimed more than 8 million lives. Some have even estimated the number to be unknown because of disease and malnutrition. Nothing like the Congo Cauldron has existed since the days of King Leopold's Rubber Wars. The scope of the pain and suffering is beyond belief. But at the heart of the situation is an interest conflict. Who shall control the wealth of one of the world's richest nations?

Fighting continues to be fuelled by the country's vast mineral wealth, with all sides taking advantage of the anarchy to plunder natural resources. External forces, those with the power to manufacture and sell guns, and those with the economic means to manipulate the ordinary citizen against his or her own interest in order to establish resource control, are at the heart of this conflict. One can see that other areas of turbulence in the DRC also have their roots in interest conflicts.

Four Conflict Spheres in Democratic Republic of the Congo

- **Enyele** rebellion in Equateur: This is an old interest conflict over fishing rights evolved into ethnic struggles for economic and political power. Some 200,000 refugees have fled violence since 2009.
- **Ugandan rebels** in the North-East: Uganda's Lord's Resistance Army (LRA) rebels remain active in its attempt to control the Northwest of DRC.
- **Rwandan rebels** in the Kivus: Hutu and Tutsi rebel militia operate in North and South Kivu. The UN oversaw a peace agreement in 2013 with the M23 Movement, which appears to be backed by Rwanda and Uganda.
- **Ituri rebels** near oil finds: North-eastern province has been quiet since a 2007 peace accord, encouraging oil firms to tap reserves in Lake Albert on Ugandan border, yet the Ituri people feel the encroachment on their lands.

Value conflicts relate to beliefs that two parties might have about life, death, the future of the universe, morality, relationships, and their place in the larger world. At the level of daily life people have their likes and dislikes. One person may believe that most humans do not want to work and therefore is critical of those who appear poverty stricken. Another person's value may be that neighbors should assist those who are less fortunate. Most value conflicts in African states are dependent upon myths, emotions, religious beliefs, philosophical outlooks, and general approaches to human behavior.

In Africa, these values conflicts are often grounded in tradition and generation and the clash of tradition with tradition generates new and dangerous realities. One argument is put forth that the tradition of a particular nation or segment of a nation is the proper one and the other tradition is an improper, even false one. This is, in its core, a religious conflict. These have proved to be much more sinister than other conflicts because the belief in a divine flag that can be waved at will to inspire allegiance often proves more capable of bringing passions to the front than culture, ethnicity, or interest. These different values orientation are major sources of African competitions. For examples of these types of conflicts one can look to the realities of fundamentalist Islamic rebellions.

Nigeria, Chad, Niger and the Boko Haram. Within the last month a joint force comprising 100 soldiers from Nigeria, Chad, and Niger confronted Islamic militants from the Boko Haram in the town of Baga, in northeast Nigeria on the shores of Lake Chad. To demonstrate that this is a value conflict one has to consider that a majority of the soldiers who intercepted the Boko Haram are Muslim themselves. However, the interpretation of Islam by contending groups of believers has the potential of creating severe challenges to African societies, leave alone the inter-religious animosity in certain sectors. Nevertheless, the ability of these religious groups to create societal problems strike at the very heart of multicultural, diverse, and pluralistic African nations. Imposition of a particular set of religious values always lead to rebellion in democratic-minded people.

Boko Haram is an Islamic group that believes politics in northern Nigeria has been seized by a group of corrupt, false Muslims.

It wants to wage a war against them, and the Federal Republic of Nigeria generally, to create a "pure" Islamic state ruled by sharia law.

Since August 2011 Boko Haram has planted bombs in public places or in churches in Nigeria's northeast. The group has also broadened its targets to include setting fire to schools. In March 2012, some twelve public schools in Maiduguri were burned down during the night, and as many as 10,000 pupils were forced out of education.

Boko Haram should not be confused with the global jihadist al-Qaeda in the Islamic North Africa, or Somalia's al Shabab. They are similar only in the fact that they believe they have the "right" interpretation of Islam and the others do not. Al-Qaeda and al-Shabab have more global ambitions than Boko Haram which is a movement against Western learning. Despite its attack on the UN compound in Abuja in August 2011, Boko Haram does not seem bent on attacking Western material interests, only Nigerians. The organization has its eyes on Nigeria's government, especially its influence in the North where girls and boys are going to school and many people are seeking a better relationship with traditional values or even Christian sentiments.

Structural conflicts refer to those conflicts that are created by the structure of the geography or climate of a region. A nation may be an island or a society may live in the desert or in a tropical forest or on top of mountains. These facts add to the structural realities around which nations can compete. At one time the United States was strangely concerned about the idea of being a two-ocean country, one that stretched from the Atlantic Ocean to the Pacific Ocean. The tension was about how to defend the Pacific Coast. This was finally put to rest after World War II and the bombing of Japan. However, geographic interests are at the root of many conflicts. If desert people want to move to agricultural areas, this will produce tension. If agrarian people want to corral and resist the encroachment of pastoralists this will produce tension. I call these structural conflicts because there is nothing that any people did to create these dramatic situations. Nature created them. For example, the threat launched a few weeks ago against Ethiopia by Egypt, Saudi Arabia, and Sudan toward Ethiopia about the waters of the Nile relate to the structural situation of the countries. Ethiopia, one would argue, has as much right to its water as any other nation. The Abay River is an Ethiopian river. An individual country never causes structural conflicts; rather, these types of conflicts are the results of factors beyond the control of any one party or nation. They may be geographical or climate related.

Sudan's Internal Conflicts. The Khartoum government is beset by wars on all sides it seems. The Nubians are protesting. The Beja are angry. The people of the Blue Nile are resisting. The South Kordofan people are distressed. The Darfurians are dislocated, degraded, and determined to be free.

In order to address this situation Khartoum will have to create a more democratic response to diversity. This will mean that the so-called Arab minority will effectively lose political power. This is not a bad solution; it is the only viable and peaceful solution to the aspirations of the vast masses of the country. Imposition works only for a short time until the people organize and rebel. Khartoum like Pretoria in the days of apartheid must look no farther than its own house to see why everyone is rebelling against the central authority.

There were facile arguments advanced at first about pastoralists and agriculturalists. This seemed reasonable on the surface as perhaps the key structural issue involved in the Darfurian war. However, pastoralists and agriculturalists have been living in proximity for centuries in Africa without major wars. What seemed different is the imposition on the Darfurian people of a cultural path that they were not prepared to take. They were Muslim, but they were Africans and their resistance was to being forced out of their own cultural frame to something else.

Thus, some conflicts in Africa bear the marks of several types in one. These hybrids are much more difficult to resolve because of their complexity. Race, ethnic expansion, and cultural imperialism must be added to the internal and external issues plaguing the African continent. We know full well how to speak of white racism in Africa but we have not yet learned the language of Arab racism in Africa. This is something different from religious domination or influence; racism exists even when both parties have the same religion. This is why the Muslim community in South Sudan thought that it was necessary for the South to separate from the North. Those southern Muslims felt the same whip, because they were African and black, that was felt by other Dinka and Nuer people. Indeed, as we will see the issue is always one of mutual respect not mutual hatred.

Like other regions, Africans conflict over many issues such as ethnic cleansing in Darfur, the impact of global warming in the riverine areas, the struggle for petroleum and minerals in poor nations, the impact of globalization, Westernization, pollution of the seas, Arabizing of traditionally African areas, massive migration of Africans to Northern Africa en route to Europe, and the militarization of children soldiers. Discussions of any of these issues normally produce divergent opinions. These are sensitive but necessary discussions for peace; solutions of substantive and enduring problems require courage. Rarely have we found in Africa a solution to our problems without the courage to speak truth to ourselves.

It is incorrect for anyone to ever assume that Africans have not been attentive to these issues despite the overpowering evidence of external intervention into most of the conflicts. Truly the African Union has sought to, among other things to:

- To defend the sovereignty, territorial integrity and independence of its Member States;

- To accelerate the political and socio-economic integration of the continent;
- To promote and defend African common positions on issues of interest to the continent and its peoples;
- To encourage international cooperation, taking due account of the Charter of the United Nations and the Universal Declaration of Human Rights;
- To promote peace, security, and stability on the continent;
- To promote and protect human and peoples' rights in accordance with the African Charter on Human and Peoples' Rights and other relevant human rights instruments.

In effect, an Africa, freed from the vestiges of colonialism in all of its dimensions, economic, philosophical, and cultural, would bring stability to the continent and remove Africa, especially in its fragmented reality as nation-states, from being a hotly contested region for international political maneuvers. Kwame Nkrumah had such a vision for Africa; one that was political but also more than political; it was also cultural and philosophical, and in his terms, *Afro-centric*.

The Structure of Peace

The structure of peace as a doctrine in world affairs has largely been left to European thinkers and politicians. We have rarely considered the possibility that African ideas are more clearly beneficial to resolving conflict. Yet it is clear that while Africans have looked to more practical examples of peace, the absence of war, and the massaging of dignity, there have been political philosophers who have proposed enterprises that create the conditions for African and world peace. The earliest African philosopher was Imhotep, the builder of the first pyramid, the world's first architect and doctor, whose very name means, "He who comes in peace." So deeply have Africans, black Africans, understood that the aim of society's leaders is to hold back chaos that they have all believed that Maat, the practice of harmony, balance, order, truth, righteousness, justice, and reciprocity, sat at the entrance to conflict resolution.

A United Geography

The African continent is one continuous landmass with several outlying islands such as Madagascar, Zanzibar, Cape Verde and smaller islands. It is a vast territory; if it were a single country, it would be the largest nation in the world. One could put Russia, the largest country in the world (17 million sq. kilometers) and Canada (10 million sq. ki) inside the continent of Africa (30.2 million sq. kilometers). Canada, the second largest country in the world, and the United States, the third largest, can fit comfortably inside Africa. You could fit the United States, India, all of Europe, including the United Kingdom inside Africa and have territory left over. Put another way, if there were a United States of Africa it would be the world's largest nation in terms of territory. It would be the third largest in terms of population after China and India.

The continent of Africa is not poor, although the people of Africa are often in poverty. Africa has enough arable land to feed the entire earth, yet in some countries people regularly confront hunger. This is what others have called the paradox of Africa: The richest land and the poorest people. Even taking into consideration the massive deserts, Sahara and Kalahari, the African continent with its extensive savannas, deep forest resources, and great arable regions could easily support the continent. It is a matter of organization of resources, not the lack of possibilities. The mineral resources of the continent are fabulous and in some ways, important instances, Africa is the richest continent on the earth. Desert minerals, grazing animals, oils for industries, petroleum, futuristic minerals for information technologies are abundant in the continent. More types of wood can be found in Africa than all the other continents combined. So why do we have so many conflicts raging on the continent of Africa at this time?

Toward a Re-Organization of Africa

Since these facts are true, how can Africa organize to take advantage of this strength? What peaceful activities are necessary to build a continental powerhouse? What Afrocentric interventions might provide avenues toward solutions on the continent? I want to introduce implementable policies and processes rather than to engage in general talk about issues.

Almost all of the problems of Africa can be traced to economic exploitation, religious tension, and cultural degradation. The decline in agricultural production in Africa over the last thirty years in most instances are tied directly to how Western nations provided, prohibited or reduced the natural competitive exporting behavior of African nations. Even today the African exports have been heavily taxed and consequently in areas such as cotton production the European and American nations have supported their own farmers and stifled competition from African farmers who have been supported by their governments. There is no lack of energy, capability, or technical know how on the part of Africa; it is strictly a lack of organizational and political power to see the continent's economic interest protected.

I am convinced that Africa must be united as one federative union. I like the title United States of Africa. This is not a foreign idea; it is an African idea. Its origins are deep in the history of the continent itself.

The First Nation

There is a history for African leadership in regard to nation-building. The first nation on earth was an African nation. The creation of Kemet was an act of the collective will of indigenous African people.

The state of Kemet was comprised of 42 ethnic groups with spiritual, mathematical, philosophical, cosmological, and agricultural similarities. Their response to nature and to human relations was something to be envied and emulated by others.

When Menes came down from the South of Kemet (Egypt) around 3400 BC, by the Africans to unite the forty-two *sepats*, called *nomes* by the Greeks, he achieved something that would have been criticized in the same way as people criticize the discussion of a united Africa. Each sepat had its own emblem, its own name for the supreme deity, its own variation on the language of the Nile Valley, its own special ethnic history, and its own capital city with its own shrines and yet Menes the Great was able to successfully achieved national status.

For example, the *sepat* called Ta Seti had as its emblem, "The Land of the Bow," its Neteru were Anuket and her mother Satis the wife of Khnum and its capital was Abu known later as Elephantine (Greek).

An African Orientation: The Four Djeds

On the whole, even when a person erred it was not conceived of as rebellion against god. The person did not commit a crime against god; the person was moving against the established order and the responsibility of one god or another was to see that the order was vindicated. The transgression was always against community, against the people, and therefore there was no guilt although shame was fundamental. In ancient Egypt as throughout ancient Africa there is no violent conflict between gods and humans; there is also no image of the individual hero standing against the people. The concept "the wrath of God" does not appear either and consequently the aberrations of the ancient Egyptians are not sinful as against god; they are the results of ignorance and the poor fellows who commit such acts must be disciplined and shamed. The truly ignorant knows neither good nor evil.

The Afrocentric Approach to Resolution

Only through knowledge of causes can a society achieve harmony, otherwise disorder and disharmony, which represent evil, dominate. Whenever disorder exists in a society or between nations or between humans and nature, we have the concept of evil, the equivalent of the existentialist's indecisiveness, the only sin. In African thought, disharmony in the community must be quickly corrected. This is why there was often a dependence on the consecration made of elements incarnated in particular animals. We sometimes speak of animal worship that, by the way, occurs nowhere that I know of in Africa. There are rhythmic meditations that were used to clarify essential functions of nature. This was not a worship of animals, but a grasping for essentiality. What is essential in the lion's courage? What constitutes the vital element in the leopard? How is the strength of the bull related to the essential quality of strength in society? What is the meaning of sacrifice in such a sense or have we forgotten how we came to the resolution of our problems prior to the coming of the invaders?

In the ancient Egyptian nation, around 3000 BC, long before the prophets Buddha, Jesus, and Mohammed, the scarab, the beetle, Khepera, as it was called, represented the expression "I shall come into existence," hence, transformation. Therein is the secret to an old, new now, pattern in human thinking. What we reach for is the source of harmony with our neighbors in order to bring about transformation.

These ideas have been developed from studying African cultural responses to family, community, and nation over a long period of time. I sought out the wisdom of the ancient people of the Nile

Valley and found the concept of Maat. I ran into the philosopher of Khunanup the eloquent peasant and discovered the source of power. I have studied the concept of the dja in Akan and the idea of iwa pele in Yoruba and so forth as an alternative to the imposition of a line of thinking inherited from Europe. There are four djeds of peaceful resolution to conflict.

Creative Engagement

African nations must choose to be outside of the ordinary. We must appeal to the ideas that create the mixture and mortar for structural peace. One way to do this is to examine the role of ancestors in a particular place or society. When I was a student studying for a communication degree one of the key components that I learned was that you must use audience analysis. This is a major concept in the field of communication. I can negotiate with you more successfully if I know something about where you came from, who are your ancestors, and what constitutes the structure of your thinking I am more apt to be able to reach you at the same place from which I view myself.

Naked Negotiation

Leave religion behind. Of course, I know that it is impossible for people to divest themselves completely of their cultural or religious back ground. These are attributes that they have grown up with and they constitute the myths that allow many people to maintain some semblance of value. Yet on the other hand when we are confronted with a possibility of catastrophic war we cannot give any nation or people the right to plunge Africa into the swamps of disaster. We must not insist that our god is better than someone else's if we are to bring about peace. Unfortunately religion is the handmaiden of more war and more deaths than any other factor in the modern world. When you combine religion with race and raw materials you have the ingredients of a unmentionable nasty conflict. All negotiations must be without religion. The recent Mali conflagration led by a series of jihadists who attacked Gao, Kidal, Timbuktu and other northern Malian cities did so in the context of religion, illegal drugs, uranium, gold, petroleum and other strategic minerals. Mali is the third largest gold producer in Africa; it has great uranium potential in the Falea area; it has diamonds in the Kayes region and it has bauxite, iron, manganese, copper, phosphate and marble. I mention this only to highlight the fact that raw materials and illegal drugs stand next to religion as factors in conflict but the problem is more complex than Ansar Dine hijacking the legitimate protests of the Tamaschek (Tuaregs) for more resources in their area. Ansar Dine brought wanton destruction to the area but they were backed and are backed by those who have money to buy guns and those who make guns. They do not make these weapons of destruction in Mali. The destruction of the sages' tombs of the Djingareyber Mosque built by Kankan Musa in 1325 should be alarming to those who adhere to fundamentalist ideas of religion. Africa has seen too much destruction of its cultural heritage; no wonder some claim that there is nothing in Africa because the destroyers' swords have shattered evidences and achievements from Egypt to Mauritania.

Thus, one of the first steps toward a peaceful solution to African problems must be the abandonment of identity wars where people are killed for not being of the "proper" religion or ethnic group. In effect, the plague of Africa is the age-old problem of identity where Sudanese of the same general history often destroy each other because they have different grandmothers or claim to have different grandmothers. When Africa is able to secure the interests of the smallest, weakest, and least politically mature nations, then it will be able to effectively bring into existence the long-awaited Pax Africana.

www.ingramcontent.com/pod-product-compliance
Lightning Source LLC
Chambersburg PA
CBHW072021110526
44592CB00012B/1394